# HOME AND CONDO DEFECTS:

## A CONSUMER GUIDE TO FAULTY CONSTRUCTION

**Thomas E. Miller**

**Rachel M. Miller**

**and**

**Matthew T. Miller**

**SEVEN LOCKS PRESS**

Santa Ana, California

Seven Locks Press
P.O. Box 25689
Santa Ana, CA 92799

**Individual Sales.** This book is available through most bookstores or can be ordered directly from Seven Locks Press at the address above.

**Quantity Sales.** Special discounts are available on quantity purchases by corporations, associations, and others. For details, contact the "Special Sales Department" at the publishers address above.

Printed in the United States of America by
DeHART's Media Services, Inc. Santa Clara, CA

*Library of Congress Cataloging-in-Publication Data*

*is available from the publisher*

ISBN 978-1-938115-00-4

Interior Design by Fusion Creative Works, Poulsbo, WA

Illustrations by: Building Analysts, San Diego, California, 619-234-8153

**The Miller Law Firm**
**800-403-3332**
**www.constructiondefects.com**

# CONTENTS

Defects, Truth, and Videotape

Let Me See What You Have

Damages as Prescribed by Law

Cost of Repairs Versus Diminution of Value

Stigma -- Or, if It Happened Before, It Could Happen Again

Attorney Fees

Expert Fees and Costs

Punitive Damages

Settlement Strategies

Jointly Retained Experts

Large Developers Who Want to Keep Their Reputations

Owner Association Settlements

Cash or Carry for Single Family Homes?

Getting it All Down

The Enforcer

Owner Association Rules

Alternative Dispute Resolution

Mediation

Arbitration

Voluntary Settlement Conferences

General Reference

A. Attorney Hiring Criteria Checklist & Online Resources

B. Twelve Most Commonly Asked Questions and Answers

C. SB 800 (Civil Code Section 895)

D. Eleven Builders' Myths

E. Top 19 Reasons Why Builders Face Construction
    Defect Lawsuits

F. Common High Rise Defects

# PREFACE

## Why We Think You Need This Handbook

We have written extensively for lawyers and other professionals as a part of our construction defect claims practice for over thirty years. Some time ago, we realized owners, owner association boards of directors, and management representatives had very little available information to aid in determining whether construction defects exist and even less on what to do when defects do exist. Realizing consumers were not being informed, we authored a few short pamphlets targeted at filling this gap. The original Consumer Guide began as an outgrowth of one of these pamphlets, *What To Do If Your House or Condo Is Defective*, which discusses twelve of the most common questions and answers about construction defects. This pamphlet is included in Appendix C.

Now on its Second Edition, this Consumer Guide maintains our goal to aid and educate homebuyers and owners, association board members, and property managers who believe there may be one or more construction defects in their home, condo, or common areas, or those who are involved in or contemplating a construction defect claim against the developer. We strive to simplify a complex legal area so that you, the reader, can gain knowledge and power.

Construction defect claims continue to rise as new projects come to the market. As the number of defect claims has grown, the law has become more complicated. Lawyers have had to expand their areas of expertise while still being able to explain to their clients, in layman's terms, what happens throughout this process. The successful construction defect lawyer must be a skillful negotiator and trial attorney; have a working knowledge of many other technical fields involved in these claims (architecture, civil engineering, geology, structural engineering, construction techniques, and cost estimating); and an understanding of new ways of solving consumer problems without always having to make use of the court system. Mediation skills and knowledge about developer insurance issues are important.

It is impossible to analyze each law as it applies. Instead, we have attempted to summarize the law so our non-lawyer readers will have a general understanding of it. To accomplish this, occasionally we re-emphasize information where there is overlap among the issues.

Please note that the purpose of this book is not to provide legal advice or direction. Our sole intention is to educate consumers by providing pertinent information about what to look for and how to work with your lawyer and the legal system in a construction defect claims process. If you believe you have a construction defect problem, you should contact a competent attorney before acting. If you have any questions or comments, you can visit The Miller Law Firm website at www.constructiondefects.com or email us at info@constructiondefects.com.

# ACKNOWLEDGMENTS

We are grateful to the many home and condominium associations who have entrusted The Miller Law Firm to represent them over the last 30 years of our practice. We never lose sight of the families that live within these communities and whose lives and livelihoods are impacted by shoddy construction practices and errant builders. We dedicate this guide to these families.

# ABOUT THE AUTHORS

*Thomas E. Miller*, the founder and president of The Miller Law Firm, has represented owners and owner association's board of directors throughout California and the Western States for over thirty years and has recovered more than $500 million dollars on their behalf. Mr. Miller received his B.A. with high honors from California State University Long Beach (1970), and his J.D. from the University of California, Hastings College of the Law (1973). A nationally recognized specialist on construction defect and land subsidence claims, Mr. Miller has written and lectured extensively on these subjects. He is the author of the only legal textbook and treatise on the subject, *California Construction Defect Litigation: Residential and Commercial* (1986 & 1993) and *Handling Construction Defect Claims: Western States* (3rd Edition, 1999; Supplemented Annually). He has been the principal speaker at extension programs tailored to educate community association managers and board members at the University of California and California State University campuses. Mr. Miller has been a featured speaker with such trade and industry groups as the Community Associations Institute (CAI), the California Association of Community Managers (CACM), the Institute of Real Estate Management (IREM), and the Executive Council of Home Owners (ECHO). He has been a featured media expert on construction defects with such national publications as the *New York Times, San Francisco Chronicle, Los Angeles Times, Orange County Register, Las Vegas Sun, The Oregonian, San Francisco and Los Angeles Daily Journal, National Geographic,* and the *National Law Journal.* He is a member of the State Bar of California, American Bar Association, American Arbitration Association, and numerous local bar associations. He is a past member of the Board of Directors of the Consumer Attorneys of California, and he is an active member of ECHO, CAI, and a founding member of CACM

*Rachel M. Miller* is the co-author of *Handling Construction Defect Claims: Western States,* (3rd Edition, 1999; Supplemented Annually), and is a partner with the Miller Law Firm. She received her B.A. from Loyola Marymount University, and her J.D. from California Western School of Law in San Diego. In her unique role with the Miller Law Firm, Ms. Miller has been featured in the *Los Angeles Times, Orange County Register* and *The Washington Post*, as well as numerous television and radio programs. Ms. Miller regularly speaks to the community association industry and at law firm practice forums about consumer legislation, disaster response, construction defects, media relations, and marketing. To further her involvement in the community association industry, she is a member of the Community Associations Institute (CAI), a past member of the elite President's Club, a founding member of California Association of Community Managers (CACM), Executive Council of Homeowners (ECHO), and the Institute of Real Estate Management (IREM). Ms. Miller has served on numerous committees and boards of these organizations, and has been honored with numerous awards by them. She has been the editor, coordinator, and moderator of several university extension programs on construction defect law for community associations, including courses at various campuses of both the University of California and California State University. Ms. Miller is a member of the California State Bar, Consumer Attorneys of California, and Legal Marketing Association.

*Matthew T. Miller* is a partner with The Miller Law Firm. He coordinates expert investigation and testing to insure all defect issues have been identified and addressed in the most cost effective manner. Matt is also a member of the research and editorial team on all firm publications and with his vision created the first web site directed solely to helping owner associations with construction defects, www.constructiondefects.com. It remains today as the signature site for The Miller Law Firm. Matt earned his B.A. in 1994 from the University of California at Berkeley. Matt went on to earn his J.D. from University of California Hastings College of the Law in 2000, and has been a member of the California State Bar since 2001. Right after law school, Matt took a year off to study abroad and earn a culinary arts degree from Le Cordon Bleu in Paris. He continued his training in San Francisco, where he worked for two of the City's preeminent chefs, followed by earning a spot to train in one of Spain's best kitchens at the restaurant Arzak in San Sebastian. He is a member of CAI, CACM and ECHO, and is co-author of The Miller Law Firm's 2nd Edition of *Home and Condo Defects: A Consumer Guide to Faulty Construction*, 2011.

# INTRODUCTION

With condominiums and houses popping up like wildflowers on what seems like every piece of space available on hillsides, in valleys, on earthquake faults, and city infill growth areas, construction defect problems are growing at an equally fast pace. The law, of course, is attempting to keep up with changing building environments, construction techniques, and consumers' changing needs. As you will see from the following chapters, construction defect claims require considerable work and effort by owners and owner associations. Why, then, is the number of construction related claims rising?

Part of the problem is just the sheer number of new developments being built in short time frames. The more units built, the more mistakes can be made. Another part of the problem is that in many communities the land most suited for housing has already been used. With the space available, builders are left with complex problems, such as, carving out hillsides or filling in valleys to build homes or tearing down old city buildings to make way for new urban infill projects. Mid- and high-rise mixed-use condominium projects bring their own set of issues, such as, exterior building materials and components being exposed to significant weather challenges. To add to these complexities, within the past few years, sustainable or "green" design, materials, and construction methods are also promising to provide long-term owner and association benefits. Doing any of this right requires care. Instead, builders frequently cut corners to save a few dollars and increase profits.

Shoddy workmanship is another reason claims are increasing. Nowadays, most condominium and housing projects are mass-produced and no longer rely on skills practiced by trained craftsman who build individually constructed homes. Focusing on profit incentives, some members of the production housing industry will quickly assemble and market a development without paying attention to detail. Mixed in with this lack of skilled workmanship and lack of attention to detail are the materials builders select, not to save money for the consumer, but often to increase profits.

After World War II, mass-produced housing became the norm to provide homes for returning veterans and their families. Builders started using galvanized piping (or worse) for plumbing, and aluminum wiring for electrical systems. Both corroded, and the aluminum wiring even caused homes to burn down. Builders failed to reinforce slabs with sufficient steel. They failed to double-check the soil to be sure it would support a house and not shift, buckle, or erode away. One builder even ran galvanized piping for natural gas through the concrete slab. The pipes rusted, leaked gas into homes, and presented potentially deadly results.

Another practice that became common and that lead to problems was the offsite production of components used in these homes. No longer did a skilled carpenter carefully build a wood window frame that perfectly fit the structure's framing. No longer did experienced masons build finely designed fireplaces. New space-age industrial external wall coverings replaced wood siding. Plumbers succumbed to plastic pipes and fittings. Roofers stopped using wood shingles or slate on well-slanted roofs. Instead, they used tar components on flat roofs, or composite roofs covered with rocks on surfaces without enough pitch or slant. Windows and doors, along with many other items, were produced in factories miles away, often with insufficient quality control and design tolerances. Today, products are being manufactured overseas where quality control is almost non-existent. These cheaper alternatives become installed in units and lead to problems for consumers.

This meant less expensive housing could be built for a mass market, but quality was sacrificed for quantity. The result was that many states decided to apply strict liability legal concepts—similar to those applied to other mass-produced products, such as automobiles—to construction defect actions. Other states increased the use of older remedies such as negligence, implied warranties, fraud, and breach of contract. And let's face facts: because of strict liability and similar claims, houses are better built, just as automobiles are safer. Today, most states have enacted laws to better define a defect and advise you when you can and can't file a lawsuit. In California, under SB 800 (California Civil Code Section 895) an association is required to provide notice to developers of any defects to allow them a chance to offer a repair before a lawsuit can be filed. For more on this statute, see Appendix D.

An additional source of problems was the rise in common interest housing. To obtain government approval, developers frequently built roadways, and to decrease public expense, deeded the ownership of these roads to the residents. Generally, the association in a master planned community owns this common interest area, along with amenities such as sidewalks, community swimming pools, tennis courts, and recreational fitness facilities. In condominiums, the association frequently owns everything except the interior air space and fixtures of individual apartment-style units. This means that for defects in these common interest areas, the association's board of directors can bring suit.

The building industry complains that construction defect actions increase the cost of housing, thereby harming its consumers. If anything, however, the claims have benefited both the consumer and the industry. The industry has had to come to grips with the inevitable, and join consumer attorneys to devise ways to better manage the litigation claim process.

Consumers benefit because developers, fearful of defect claims, build better housing. Builders pay more attention to soils tests, roofing techniques, materials selection, sustainable practices, and other factors, which increases housing quality without significantly increasing costs. Builders have also implemented quality control programs and published maintenance manuals to help association boards and consumers. When builders fail to build to a higher standard, there are remedies available so consumers can get what they paid for.

Still, some never learn. One builder used regular nails instead of galvanized roofing nails to save a few pennies. When the nails corroded, the roof leaked, the sub-roofing and framing began to rot, and the developer ended up paying millions of dollars to replace all the roofs in the development. It's safe to say that on the next project, the builder spent those few extra pennies on the correct nails to save millions of dollars in repair costs down the road. The builder who learns from past mistakes and pays stricter attention to those details in future projects will have a better chance to rebuild a good reputation and sell their units faster. Undoubtedly, the smart builders who hear of these problems encountered by others will also take more care in their construction, thus enabling them to sell their products quickly as well.

Governments have tried to keep pace by raising building standards, requiring more complete building inspections by better trained inspectors, and setting up a more effective pre-construction approval process. This also created a more consumer-friendly environment and helped increase both housing availability and quality. But resources in boom times become strained by an increase in the amount of demand for new construction and good intentions give rise to fewer inspections and more defects.

Construction defect claims have also helped bring attention to health problems by poor quality building. Exposure to mold and other products and materials used in the construction of the home or condo can lead to health complications known as "sick building syndrome", which causes people to suffer a variety of conditions from mild allergic reactions to chronic and debilitating illnesses. As a result of laws that protect the homebuyer and streamline the construction defect claim process, builders are more careful to build homes that eliminate or significantly reduce the risk of such exposure.

Often, developers knew about the problems caused by exposure to mold and certain building materials and said nothing to consumers, which is tantamount to fraud. Again, defect claims encouraged developers to avoid building in such a way as to cause these problems to occur in the first place and to properly notify consumers when these conditions are present, thus avoiding costly, reputation damaging claims.

As you can see—and as this book explains—construction defect claims have improved American housing. We hope the building industry will work with consumer groups to continue this trend. More work remains to be done.

# CHAPTER ONE: THE BIG PICTURE

## A Capsule Version of How It Works

As a rule of thumb in California, owners of new homes or condos can pursue a claim for construction defects within 10 years of substantial completion. After 10 years, your options are much more limited. A home or condo is the largest investment most people make in a lifetime, but it is more than just an investment. To nearly everyone, a home is where you raise your children, build a life, and attempt to fulfill the American Dream.

To many, the American Dream turns into a nightmare when, after years of saving for a down payment, they discover their newly purchased home is filled with defects such as, leaky roofs and windows, cracked walls and foundations, flooding, or an entire building is settling and shrinking. Luckily, laws governing faulty construction have evolved from the old *caveat emptor* (let the buyer beware). Today's laws include numerous ways for consumers to recover losses caused by construction defects in both residential property and commercial buildings. An important legal development is for courts to apply to homebuyers the consumer protections that used to apply only to automobile purchasers. It was not until 1974 that California courts ruled that homeowners had an implied warranty of "fitness for a particular use," meaning if you bought a house, you should be able to live in it comfortably, and maintain its property value, even if you are not the original buyer. Nearly all states have followed in creating these protections for owners and owner associations, although usually the only way to enforce your rights is through the civil court system with the assistance of a lawyer. This means timely pursuing a construction defect claim to enforce one's rights.

One construction defect claim can involve dozens of responsible parties. Today, developers, builders, contractors, subcontractors, construction managers, apartment converters, lenders, architects, engineers, and other trade and professionals can be involved in one lawsuit. While a construction defect claim may appear simple at first glance, these claims involve confronting a wide array of legal issues.

This, of course, means that resolving a construction defect claim requires a law firm with lawyers who possess considerable legal and organizational skills, and has the ability to finance the entire construction defect claim process. It also means that lawyers involved in construction defect cases must know their way around several very technical design and construction fields. They must also know who are the best experts in dozens of disciplines and be aware which expert best suits a particular situation. A law firm that specializes its practice in construction defect claims should be your preferred choice. Those that profess to be a full service community association firm often fall short of needed litigation and negotiation skills to efficiently resolve a construction defect claim.

Over the years, city and other local governments have entered the fray. Because of construction defect claims, governmental entities have drafted better regulations, and tightened the enforcement of those that already exist. Local governments now require developers to make certain modifications to conform to particular geographic and geotechnical situations. For example, housing in areas subject to earthquakes may be required to meet certain standards in order to better withstand tremors. In California's Central Valley, water may not naturally drain, and, as a result, foundations retain liquids as if they were giant sponges. Therefore, special water intrusion protection and drainage systems may have to be installed.

In other areas, the soil may consist primarily of clay. Expansion and contraction of the clay can result in cracked foundations. In those cases, building codes may require special steel reinforcement within the concrete slabs. Additionally, deserts, mountains, coastal ocean bluffs, bays, and sand dunes demand special building techniques. Extreme temperature variations, snowfall, or high amounts of wind-driven rain should require architectural changes to standard plans in order to fit the specific environment in which a development is being built.

What constitutes a construction defect is wide-ranging and can also include environmental issues. The presence of hazardous chemicals, earthquake faults, toxic molds, termites, inadequate drainage, leaking roofs, bad plumbing, faulty wiring, cracked slabs, structural failures, electrical problems, safety code violations, defective furnaces, siding and stucco failure, failing foundations, poorly constructed sidewalks and roadways, poor soil compaction, hidden landslides and otherwise unstable soil, "sick building syndrome" causing materials, and many other problems all can be considered "defects." The Americans with Disabilities Act of 1990 might be involved in claims regarding commercial buildings and apartments. Almost anything that can go wrong probably will go wrong, and can be a "defect."

In California, SB 800 (Civil Code Section 895) was passed by the Legislature and went into effect January 1, 2003. This statute completely changed the landscape on how defect claims are processed. The law clearly defines what constitutes a construction defect and imposes several new time limitations within which to bring a specific defect claim. For more on this statute, see Appendix D. Passage of SB 800 and its new time limitations created a more urgent need for owners or an owner association's board of directors to act in a timely fashion. Failure to bring a claim within the statutory period creates a situation in which options become limited and the right to pursue a claim may be lost forever.

Most homes or condos built today belong to common interest developments that typically own the development's common areas, including mechanical rooms, parking garages, elevators, pathways, swimming pools, decks, and roadways. The owner association's Board of Directors is usually involved in bringing the construction defect claim forward. California Civil Code, §1365.7 creates a fiduciary duty upon each board member to investigate alleged defects and timely pursue these claims.

The owner association's board members must be educated and guided through this complex process. The board should understand its fiduciary duty, what could happen to the association members if they fail to timely bring a claim, and the critical path to pursuing a construction defect claim, including how it may impact sales and financing, or refinancing for the association members.

First, defects must be discovered and analyzed. Next, an involved prelitigation statutory process, like those found in the above-mentioned SB 800 (Civil Code Section 895), must be satisfied. Once litigation begins, homes or condos, and common areas will be inspected and tested and documents exchanged. Depositions by the opposing parties may ensue and the production of what can be hundreds of association and development documents is commonplace. Attorneys then prepare the case for settlement, mediation, and other forms of case resolution. In less than five percent of cases, trial is necessary.

Before and after the case is resolved, board decisions regarding how the settlement funds are used and how the property is to be repaired must be made. This typically involves the board, the management company, the association's architect, re-construction companies, and the input from different experts and consultants. When repairs are made, the board will have to supervise the efforts and will be required to help coordinate the various parties involved.

What damages a party can recover can include monetary compensation for repairs, actual repairs made, loss of use, relocation expenses, expert and consultant fees, or even having the developers buy back the homes or condos where repairs are not appropriate, e.g., a landslide area. In the case of a common interest development, this can easily total millions of dollars.

The purpose of this handbook is to help you navigate this legal quagmire. The construction defect claim process is not easy, but you have only one shot at saving your largest investment.

## Chapter One Do's and Don'ts
### Do:

- Do be on the lookout for defects when inspecting the property for purchase.
- Do remember defects can result from any number of design and construction problems.
- Do retain counsel's advice before hiring experts.
- Do retain an independent and qualified home inspector before purchasing a property.
- Do read any builder warranty carefully. You'll be surprised what it does not cover.
- Do, as an association board member, undertake a proper due diligence analysis of the situation and consult with experienced counsel, man-

agement representatives, and experts before you begin a dialogue with the builder. Board members have a fiduciary duty to association members.

## Don't:

- Don't take the developer's word for construction quality.
- Don't be lulled into a false sense of security by clever developers who advise that the problems are normal.
- Don't forget to notify your owner association's board of directors about potential defects.

# CHAPTER TWO: JUST WHAT ARE THESE DEFECTS, ANYWAY?

Lawyers and courts seem to use different dictionaries than most when talking about most things, including construction defects. Some courts have said the consumer must be able to rely on the skill of the developer to build in a "reasonably workmanlike manner," which seems to mean the builder should use the necessary skill and knowledge to build a project well. Failing to comply with this concept is referred to as "negligence."

In a negligence action, the association's board must show what the developer did wrong and, more importantly, that the developer had breached a duty it had to the owner association and said breach caused damages. For example, suppose that because a developer used the wrong size or kind of nails a home's siding fails. The association must show that the siding failed because the developer used the wrong sized nails, had a duty to use the correctly sized nail, and by using the wrong nails the siding failed prematurely causing damage to the property. Lawyers analyze negligence with terms like "proximate cause", "cause in fact", and what a "reasonable person" would say. This can be a confusing and difficult process to understand for an association board member. It all simply translates to, "I have a problem in my home, unit, or common area, the builder did something wrong, and I want it fixed!"

In California, "strict liability" can be used against a developer who is a "mass producer of housing, and places them into the stream of commerce." The person who wants to bring a claim need only show that there is some sort of defect. What all of this means is that if a developer builds traditional homes or low-, mid-, or high-rise condos, that are to be sold and resold, an owner association may bring a claim by simply showing a defect exists.

In recent years, urban centers, warehouse districts, and downtown areas with unused buildings have been given new life by converting them to condos. Developers use older, and in many cases, unique facades, while reconstructing a lot of the building components to meet today's standards. In some instances, developers will take newer buildings intended as office space and turn them into condominiums. The consumer should know that these types of buildings follow a different path for construction defects. Courts will not apply strict liability, and the legislature has not set standards for these types of units, thus, a developer's liability for condo conversions is not clearly defined.

Instead, your legal recourse when defects are discovered in a condo conversion is to file suit for negligent and intentional misrepresentation and non-disclosure. When a conversion occurs in a building under 10 years from its initial completion, an opportunity may be provided to name the original builder. Generally speaking, the buildings used for conversion are older buildings, and the developer who converted the building will be the entity you name in your lawsuit.

In a construction defect claim involving a conversion, your best chance of recovery is derived from what the builder touched during the conversion process. For example, if the developer installed a new roof and windows, that later on leak, you may recover to repair these. A more difficult question is what should the developer have done when converting a building? For example, if the developer inspected and left old plumbing in place, and later that plumbing causes damage, is the developer liable? Questions like this are left up to the court to decide. Condominium conversions will require additional analysis of the association CC&R's, purchase documents, maintenance records, developer files, and Department of Real Estate documents to see what should have been disclosed. Failure to disclose can be helpful, but is not a silver bullet.

The scope of a construction defect claim is not limited to just faulty workmanship under legal theories of negligence or strict liability. A developer should do what is necessary to stop a problem from ever occurring. In one case, a developer built nearly 200 condos on a beautiful bluff overlooking the Pacific Ocean. If the bluffs eroded, the homes could have fallen into the water. The courts said this was a defect and the developer was required to take the protective measure of reinforcing the bluff. Developers building in cities with a known history of earthquakes are responsible to erect high-rise condominiums to withstand an earthquake up to a certain size. Failure to do so can be considered a construction defect.

As you have just read, what constitutes a defect in construction is not always clear. Subtle legal standards, who is the developer, or what type of building you purchased all play an important role in determining your rights. In California, the legislature provided significant clarity as to what constitutes a construction defect by enacting SB 800 (Civil Code Section 895, See Appendix C). It is important to note that this legislation applies to homes or condos that signed purchase and sale agreements after January 1, 2003, and will not apply to condo conversions.

## The Patent or Latent Controversy Gives Way to New Legislative Protections

In the past, construction defects were often said to be either "patent" (things you should see) or "latent" (things you can't see). These are legal terms which lawyers can spend hours fighting over. The distinction was very important for years because it determined how much time you have for bringing suit. A patent defect is usually defined as a defect "that is apparent by reasonable inspection" with "ordinary care and prudence." For example, flooding common areas, or roofs that leak when it rains.

A latent defect is one that is "not apparent by reasonable inspection." For example, homebuyers cannot see rotting framing inside the walls or mold and usually don't know about it until the damage is already done.

These two legal theories still have teeth, but the California legislature has taken some of the arguments away from attorneys with SB 800 (Civil Code Section 895, See Appendix C). This law not only lists what constitutes a defect, but it has also created different time limitations within which a claim must be brought. Depending on the defect, a claim must be brought within 1, 2, 4, 5, or 10 years from the date of substantial completion or the date when the builder relinquishes control over the association's ability to decide when to initiate a claim, which ever is later.

## Is it a Defect or Did I Fail to Maintain it?

Although just about anything can be a defect, owners and owner associations have a responsibility to maintain their property. Developers cannot be sued because a property was not kept in good repair. For example, the owner cannot allow roof gutters to clog up with leaves and then sue because the gutters don't function properly. Maintaining the property usually is the responsibility of either an owner or the owner association, depending on the particular situation.

Deciding whether something is the result of poor maintenance or is a defect can be a tough call. Did the gutters fail to drain because the owner failed to clear the leaves, or was it because the developer incorrectly installed the gutter system? To determine this, your lawyer will probably hire an expert who will carefully review the situation and present an opinion.

## It's a Defect, but Who is Responsible?

The developer is the first answer, but others may also be responsible. If a window leaks, the developer is ultimately responsible because he produced and sold the house or condo. But if the windows were not manufactured correctly, the manufacturer is also responsible. Perhaps the same windows were incorrectly installed. The general contractor who supervised the installation and the framing subcontractor who installed it will also share responsibility.

Property managers at the time certain issues arise may be targets of legal action. Usually, they are hired by associations to manage budgets, collect dues, recommend maintenance personnel, and perform other operational matters. If they are negligent in these tasks, or fail to recognize and recommend that the board investigate potential common area construction defects, they can be held liable. Many times an owner association will indemnify a property manager under a written agreement, and the responsibility to investigate and bring a claim will shift to the owner association's board of directors. The point here is to take the necessary steps to protect your property when a potential claim exists.

Also, because owner associations hold and control owners' monies (and since the developer usually creates the owner association and sits on its first board of directors), they have a fiduciary duty, which is a much higher duty than an ordinary standard of care. The association is required to act by investigating alleged defects, and timely pursuing a claim for existing defects. The board should consult with and take the advice of qualified counsel. The breach of a fiduciary duty usually involves gross mismanagement, self-dealing, lack of business judgment, or a conflict of interest. For example, if a board was to let the statutes of limitations lapse before bringing a claim for defects this may be a breach of fiduciary duty. Also, if one shows a breach was intentional, one can receive punitive damages, which are special damages designed to punish the offender.

Breach of fiduciary duty, developer liability and insurance, and board of directors' responsibilities can become very complex. For example, the developer has the duty after selling homes or condos to not change construction aspects that could reduce the homebuyers' investments in later development phases.

Additional potential defendants are building inspectors and other governmental entities and agents. The historic rule is that governments are immune from lawsuits. But if the government installed a faulty drainage system on a hillside development, failed to properly maintain that system, and a bluff failed causing damage to buildings or homes in the area, the government is liable. If the building inspector, however, missed finding a defect during construction, they have immunity.

Law schools teach entire courses on governmental liability. What you, the consumer, need to know is that time is of the essence when a construction defect is suspected, that, generally, government entities are not potential defendants, and that all government and building department records and reports should be reviewed by an attorney.

## Chapter Two Do's and Don'ts

### Do:

- Do have your lawyer's retained consultant explain to you in simple and clear terms the type and nature of any defect.
- Do have the lawyer retain experts to demonstrate the defects.
- Do notify your lawyer and owner association of any suspected defect. What appears at first to be a minor problem could develop into a serious one later.
- Do remember that not all defects can be easily seen. Some are hidden behind walls, on roofs, or under floor coverings.
- Do carefully maintain your property. Perform an annual checkup.

- Do remember that many people and entities are potential defendants.
- Do remember to be vigilant and act timely to bring a formal complaint.

## Don't:

- Don't release anyone before you know all of the facts and without consulting an attorney.
- Don't assume that just because a defect can't be seen that one does not exist, for example, stucco stains, mold, or unpleasant odors can be signs of defects.
- Don't attempt to analyze potential defects. That is a job for your lawyer and experts.
- Don't hesitate to inform your lawyer, property manager, or association board members of potential defects. Because of complex statutes of limitations, if you don't pursue that claim on time, you may loose that right forever.
- Don't just send a letter to your builder claiming defects as that may trigger statutes of limitations that could impact your claim.

# CHAPTER THREE:
# THE INVESTIGATION

Once defects are suspected, experts (usually called consultants at this stage, but the terms are used interchangeably) are hired. They should be hired through your lawyer to allow information produced by your expert to fall under the protection of the attorney client privilege. If you hire them directly, instead of through your attorney, the results of their investigations may have to be turned over to the developer and you might trigger various statutes of limitations, which could destroy or diminish the value of your case.

Your expert's job is to discover what your defects are and what is causing them. This can get expensive. The first thing your expert will do is walk through the development to uncover and record potential deficiencies. Photographs will do just fine in this exercise.

Experienced construction defect law firms have developed specialized techniques allowing experts to discover information as efficiently as possible. A law firm should have a well-developed working relationship with experienced and tested independent experts, and should know which experts perform best in particular situations. Not all experts are created equal, and even experts in the same field will have differing sub-areas of expertise within that field. For example, one geotechnical expert may be more experienced in analyzing earthquake problems than another, who works better in the area of landslides, slope movement, or foundation settlement. Some roofing experts are more experienced in discussing large, flat roofs on high-rise buildings, while another may be better with sloped or pitched roofs on houses. Some stucco experts are better equipped to evaluate EIFS (single coat system) failures than the traditional three-coat application.

To cut costs and save time (both of which are important goals), in multi-unit developments, experts frequently ask that confidential surveys originating in your attorney's office be sent to owners and residents to pinpoint specific problems inside the units that may be caused by common area defects. In addition, your experts and attorney will examine numerous documents, such as your board of director's minutes, developer sales and advertising materials, correspondence with other lawyers and with the developer, building inspectors' reports, and repair and maintenance records to help determine the existence of a defect, its nature, its cause, and its extent. After analyzing the surveys, the expert will conduct further interior and exterior site inspections as well as focused intrusive testing to determine what the defects are and how extensive they are throughout the development.

## Who the Experts Are

- For every defect, there seems to be a different expert. The experts you may require include:
- Architects to look at the overall construction, design, and building performance
- Structural engineers to examine load-carrying capability of walls, columns, and other structural elements
- Soils (geotechnical) engineers to report on the ground, soils, and site selection and settlement problems
- Roofing, decking, and waterproofing experts to look for leaks
- Civil engineers to check out the site grading, gutters, sidewalks, and boundary surveys, along with roads, sewage, and water delivery
- Environmental engineers to look for toxic fumes, waste, and other dangerous environmental factors
- Indoor industrial hygienists to detect "sick building syndrome" and mold
- Mechanical engineers to investigate heating, ventilating, air conditioning, and plumbing
- Electrical engineers to watch for electrical and lighting defects and failures
- Licensed general contractors and cost estimators to determine the cost to fix it all
- Your case may require other experts and sub-specialists who should be retained as needed

## HOME AND CONDO DEFECTS

In single-family home cases, it is economical to band together with as many owners as possible to share the costs of experts. Attorneys often can and will advance these costs, but you should understand that, ultimately, you are responsible for them.

Your attorney should carefully explain to you the expected costs and the types of experts that will most likely be retained. Usually, the agreement is reduced to a written contract so that everyone involved will fully understand their rights and responsibilities. Even though expert fees are recoverable by a prevailing party, your attorney should use reasonable care to keep these fees under control. Of course, when an expert is needed, he or she should be retained. You can be sure of one thing: the developer's insurance company will hire a team of experts to contest your case.

### The Property Manager's Role

If an owner association is involved, the association's property manager often plays an important role in the litigation. This, however, usually takes more time than the management company's normal duties of collecting membership dues, soliciting bids for maintenance, preparing budgets, arranging association meetings, and otherwise managing the property. Many of these extra duties mean additional costs. Among the roles the property manager can assume are:

- Identifying maintenance records
- Scrutinizing repair invoices
- Reviewing owner repair requests
- Protecting and directing information received about the case
- Making sure the property is properly maintained while the case progresses
- Arranging and running monthly or bi-monthly meetings to deal with owner complaints
- Arranging emergency or temporary repairs
- Attending owner and board meetings
- Holding special association meetings regarding litigation
- Educating new board members and officers about the litigation
- Handling proxy solicitations for loans
- Attending settlement or mediation conferences

- Taking calls from buyers, escrow companies, brokers, and agents
- Monitoring special maintenance procedures during litigation
- Accounting for additional time needed to deal with experts and other lawsuit-related matters and expenses
- Interviewing reconstruction contractors with the board
- Helping to relocate owners to temporary housing during needed repairs
- Maintaining a disclosure binder for owners and buyers

Depending on the association and its contract with the management company, these duties will exceed normal management fees. The board of directors should be prepared to pay for these extra services. You can limit many of these costs if you choose your construction defect attorney from a law firm that has the staff and experience to perform the additional tasks otherwise left to the management company.

Usually, the developer retains the association's first management company. Once owners dominate the association board of directors, it is probably a good idea for the board to approach the management company, especially if construction defect problems are evident. The board of directors should be sure that the management company has experience in working with owner associations involved in claims against developers and understands and is aware of the nature and extent of its responsibilities.

An important concept for owners and owner associations to understand as they take over board of director responsibilities is California's SB 800 (Civil Code Section 895) time limitations do not begin ticking until after the developer relinquishes control of the board. Your management company should be aware of this and what it means to the association. For more information on SB 800, see Appendix C.

## Types of Defects

Lawyers and experts frequently use very technical words to define defects, which has created some confusion over the years. Passage of California Senate Bill 800 (Civil Code Section 895) led to sweeping changes in California's laws for construction defect cases. Statutory definitions of actionable defects are established in Civil Code Section 896, with Civil Code Section 897 being a "catch all" for anything causing damage that is not specifically defined in 896. SB 800 (Civil Code Section 895) relates to construction defects for homes and condos where signed sales agreements occurred on or after January 1, 2003. For more information about SB 800 (Civil Code Section 895), see Appendix C.

Below is a list of these defects organized by their accompanying statute of limitations:

## 1 year

- Noise (from original occupancy of adjacent unit)
- Fit and finish warranty
- Irrigation and drainage
- Manufactured products

## 2 years

- Decay of untreated wood posts
- Landscaping systems
- Dryer ducts

## 4 years

- Plumbing and sewer
- Electrical
- Cracks in exterior hardscape, pathways, driveways, landscape, sidewalls, sidewalks, patios
- Corrosion of steel fences

## 5 years

- Deterioration of building surfaces due to paint or stain

## 10 years

- All other defects or violation of building standards
- Air Conditioning in living spaces
- Balconies and balcony systems
- Ceramic tile and tile backing
- Ceramic tile and tile countertops
- Decks and deck systems

- Doors
- Exterior stairs and stair systems
- Exterior stucco, siding, walls, framing, finishes and fixtures
- Fire Protection
- Foundation systems and slabs
- Foundations, load bearing components, slabs and underlying soils
- Hardscape, paths, patios, irrigation systems, landscape systems and drainage systems
- Heating
- Plumbing lines, sewer lines and utility lines
- Retaining and site walls, associated drainage systems
- Roofing materials
- Roofs, roofing systems, chimney caps and ventilation
- Shower and bath enclosures
- Soils and engineered retaining walls
- Structure
- Windows, patio doors, deck doors and related system

## What Went Wrong, and Why?

Experts attempt to discover not only what is defective but also, why it is defective. For example, a home or condo owner may notice a wall or ceiling stain. The owner thinks it is a sign of a defect, but does not know whether it is caused by a roof, deck, plumbing, window, or skylight failure. Another example is using materials in high-rise construction that have traditionally been used only on single family or low-rise construction. An expert will be able to help determine whether the right materials were selected. (For a more detailed discussion of Common High Rise Defects, see Appendix F.)

Diagnosing the cause of a problem requires considerable skill. Sometimes it is similar to determining the cause of an automobile engine malfunction. Six people can listen to an engine and come up with six different possible explanations for it, all of which are wrong. An expert mechanic can listen to the engine, run a few tests, plug it into a computer, and tell the owner what is wrong with the engine and how much it will cost to repair. The expert mechanic may initially cost more, but in the long run will be less expensive because of the mechanic's accuracy. As a mechanic friend of ours says, "I get paid $2 to tighten a bolt, but $50 to know which bolt to tighten and the best way to tighten it."

The expert may have to investigate the local building codes and national or regional construction industry standards, as they existed at the time of construction. The developer may have met the codes but did not follow industry standards. The builder's failure to meet building code requirements is good evidence of a defect, although you need to have other information as evidence to prove your damages. Remember building codes only provide the absolute minimum construction standards.

### Exactly What are "Damages"?

Damages are any physical problems directly or indirectly related to the defects. These are termed "resultant damages" and include hidden damages. A good example is defective roofing. It is apparent that a leak discolored the walls and flooded the living room. However, the leak also may have resulted in rotting the wood framing or structural beams.

Sometimes, to find all the resultant damages, parts of the common areas or owners' units must be tested. This is called "invasive" or "destructive" testing. Of course, these tests should be limited because of the inconvenience and costs involved. Testing about twenty percent of randomly selected homes or condos in an affected phase or building generally will be enough.

### How to Fix It

The experts or consultants next make repair suggestions and provide them to your attorney. These recommendations are usually very specific, and will include the repair plan or drawings, particular materials needed, scope of the work to be done, the types of workers or professionals needed, and any other information necessary to a contractor for making a responsible cost estimate.

Receiving an accurate repair cost estimate is a vital part of the resolution of any construction defect claim. It is equally important not to underestimate or overestimate and "gold plate" any repair cost. Gold plating will cause a loss of credibility with everyone involved and provide the opposition with an easily identifiable set of facts to undermine your case. It also can delay early settlement opportunities.

Determining what constitutes "gold plating" varies with the techniques used for the original construction and the quality of the original materials. For example, a common area asphalt roof that leaks because of poor installation probably cannot lead to a demand that the roof be replaced with a more expensive concrete tile one. The consumer does, however, have the right to a properly installed asphalt roof that does not leak. However, if the original materials themselves were defectively manufactured or are discontinued, the consumer probably has the right to have the roof replaced with better-proven materials, even if they are somewhat more expensive.

It is, therefore, imperative that your construction defect attorney be familiar with repair cost estimates and respected cost estimators. Even a small repair cost mistake can destroy your credibility and impact your ability to recover enough money to fix the problems responsibly.

## Chapter Three Do's and Don'ts

### Do:

- Do always hire your experts and consultants through your attorney. Otherwise, you could lose confidentiality and trigger time limit defenses.
- Do give your attorney every bit of documentation that may be even remotely related to a defect.
- Do familiarize yourself with the numbers and types of experts that may be required.
- Do promptly fill out and respond to any forms or surveys your attorney or experts may send to you.
- Do familiarize yourself with your maintenance responsibilities and the responsibilities of your owner association. Read your CC&R's (Covenants, Codes, and Restrictions) and maintenance manuals.

### Don't:

- Don't forget you may be responsible for your experts' fees and costs. Get a preliminary budget from your attorney before you start. The fees are recoverable.
- Don't attempt to analyze the nature and cause of your problems yourself. This is why experts are hired.

# CHAPTER FOUR: WHAT THE CONSUMER SHOULD WATCH FOR

While it is the experts' jobs to find, define, and estimate repair costs, there are items consumers should monitor. It is nearly impossible to list everything, but we are providing a general list below, under "Signs of Defects". If you notice or suspect a potential defect, you should notify either your property manager or your association's board of directors. You should be able to determine if the defect is the responsibility of the association by examining the Covenants, Conditions, and Restrictions (CC&R's) and condo plan. Look specifically for association and owner maintenance responsibilities sections.

Reading these documents can be a challenging process. The developer's attorney writes them in very technical "legalese", which is often indecipherable to non-lawyers and even to lawyers who do not practice in the area. Your association's property manager may be able to provide insight. Many different legal issues could be written into a set of CC&R's and a careful reading is required. Indeed, it is probably a good idea to have a qualified attorney review these documents before purchasing a home.

## First Steps To Resolution

In a common interest development, it is the association, through the board of directors, who must bring a claim for construction defects within the common areas. An owner or resident should immediately notify the association board and property manager in writing when a defect is suspected. The association must take these notices seriously because of their fiduciary duty to investigate and bring a claim for defects when they exist. The property manager should remind the association of their need to act in the best interest of those they represent. Failure to act within certain time limitations will cause the association to forever loose their right to bring a claim for certain construction defects. Another way to put it is if you miss the deadline, your lawsuit immediately fails.

## Signs of Defects

Among the items to watch for are:

- Any sign of moisture or water leakage inside your home
- Dry rot or wet rot anywhere
- Windows or doors that do not open or close correctly
- Ponding water near foundations of your home or building
- Cracks or separation in drywall, floor coverings, and concrete slabs or foundations
- External stucco cracking, flaking, or staining
- Lights that flicker on and off or overloaded circuits
- Loose, slipping, or falling roof tiles
- Water seeping up through the slab
- Uneven or sloping floors, or walls out of plumb
- Mold or mildew on drywall or around openings in buildings
- Stains or cracks on walls or ceilings
- Decks that don't drain properly, feel spongy, or have cracks on the surface.
- Concrete slabs that crack, have efflorescence, or begin to disintegrate
- Concrete block walls with efflorescence or moisture seeping through
- Balcony railings that are loose, rusting, or rotting
- Corroding metal or mechanical systems
- Patio or podium decks cracking, not draining, or show signs of efflorescence
- Irrigation systems that cause flooding or water ponding
- Wet slabs or moisture in crawl spaces
- Roofs that leak or pond water
- Windows, sliding glass doors, or skylights that leak and cause cracking or water stains
- Openings in attic crawl spaces between units; lack of fire protection between units

## Should You Tell the Developer?

In California, statutory pre-litigation laws, such as California's Calderon Process (Civil Code 1375) and SB 800 (Civil Code Section 895) right to repair laws require the owners or the association to notify the builder about the defects. This provides the developer an opportunity to investigate the complaint and fix the problem. Commonly, developers will offer a less than satisfactory fix that covers the visual problem without ever getting at the root cause of the defect. They also understand that these defects are serious and use this time to develop defenses and notify the subcontractors. So don't expect the developer to open his checkbook, pay the claim, or propose a responsible and permanent repair. To read more about these statutory pre-litigation procedures, visit our website at www.constructiondefects.com.

## The Builder Warranty Myth

Many times, builders and developers represent that they are providing a complete warranty for the home. Most likely, this is not true. Seldom do these warranties provide complete protection, and they usually have very short expiration dates.

The important thing to remember is not to take the builder's word on what the warranty covers and doesn't cover, and to realize that your legal rights far exceed what the builder's warranty provides. For more on this issue, see Appendix D. Many consumers, upon discovering a defect, will read their warranty and based upon that warranty decide that either the warranty has expired or does not cover whatever defect they suspect. Don't fall into this trap. If you suspect a defect, consult your attorney to find out if redress exists. Don't just rely on what the developer tells you. Often, the advice given will lead you to believe that the warranty does not cover whatever defect it is, when, in fact, the law may allow for a wide array of compensation possibilities. As the proverbial "ounce of prevention", it might be a good idea for you to have your attorney read the warranty and all purchase documents before you close the deal on a new home.

## Binding Arbitration Provisions in CC&R's

CC&R's frequently contain binding arbitration provisions. This means that if you have a dispute with the developer over a construction defect, you may be forced to have the matter heard and decided by an arbitrator rather than by a judge in court. Recent court decisions in California have found most of these arbitration provisions unenforceable and to one-sided.

## Maintenance Manuals and Repair Requirements

Owners and owner associations in common interest developments must comply with the maintenance responsibility laid out in SB 800 (Civil Code Section 895). Locating the maintenance obligations is the first hurdle. Typically, these are found in the CC&R's or under an Exhibit to the CC&R's that provide explanations of how various building components are to be maintained. These should also discuss whether an item is to be maintained by the association or by the owners. Generally speaking, owners maintain the airspace in their units or components that only serve their unit and the owner associations maintain the common areas.

Section 907 of SB 800 clearly discusses owner and owner associations maintenance responsibility:

> "A homeowner is obligated to follow all reasonable maintenance obligations and schedules communicated in writing to the homeowner by the builder and product manufacturers, as well as commonly accepted maintenance practices."

Section 945.5(c) of SB 800 provides the developer a defense to Section 907:

> "A builder…may be excused, in whole or in part, from any obligation, damage, loss, or liability if the builder….can demonstrate…(c) To the extent it is caused by the homeowner…of their failure to follow the builder's or manufacturer's recommendations, or commonly accepted homeowner maintenance obligations. In order to rely upon this defense as it relates to a builder's recommended maintenance schedule, the builder shall show that the homeowner had written notice of these schedules and recommendations and that the recommendations and schedules were reasonable at the time they were issued."

When the association is a mid or high-rise building, maintaining the components that make up the structure are complicated. Many times, developers draft maintenance manuals that are detailed, technical, and difficult to understand. Not following through or misunderstanding this document provides the developer with an opening to shift the discussion away from the defective condition and towards the issue of whether or not the building was properly maintained. Property managers and owner associations need to understand the severity of this issue and not following through could cost hundreds of thousands, if not millions of dollars, in a construction defect claim. A failure to maintain defense will be used vigorously by the developer and its insurance company.

In some instances, the developer provided the association with a maintenance manual that is "off the shelf", meaning these documents have not been tailored to the specific project our building components. Another inherent problem is the cost to an owner association to implement the maintenance manual. For example, if a maintenance manual calls for a yearly inspection the association may have to hire architects, engineers, and other construction or design consultants. The cost could be upwards or $25,000-$30,000 to produce such a report. Developers who fail to include the real costs into the approved DRE (Department of Real Estate) budget will force an owners association to ask it's members to pay more dues. Off the shelf documents and over-burdensome costs create unreasonable hurdles for associations trying to comply with maintenance manual obligations.

Most people who buy a home or live in a common interest development do not have the knowledge and background it takes to read a maintenance manual, understand what it means, and how to follow it. It is an overwhelming document, however, it does create long lasting obligations. Have your lawyer review it to see if, in the first place, the requirements are reasonable, and then to determine whether the owners association followed the guidelines adequately. Your lawyer can work with the appropriate consultant to establish the suitability of the manual and association compliance. Do not ignore these requirements without first doing your due diligence as suggested.

## Monthly Assessments

In common interest developments, whether the homes are freestanding single homes or condos, members are billed monthly by the association. These fees are not optional. If you fail to pay them, liens can be placed, and, potentially, your home could be sold to recoup the assessment arrearages.

An association uses the funds to keep common areas in good repair and to pay other expenses, such as, insurance costs, accounting, or management fees. Indeed, the assessment may be increased to make emergency repairs before or during litigation, or to otherwise specially fund litigation. If an association fails to bring a timely claim, the cost to make repairs to defective conditions will also fall on the association and its members through higher assessments.

Every state requires damages to be "mitigated" by doing what is reasonable to prevent a condition from getting worse. Known damages can be mitigated by performing reasonable repairs. For example, should a leak occur during litigation, a reasonable repair may be as simple as caulking an area to stop the water from entering the building. This temporary repair is sufficient because the damage was mitigated by immediately stopping the water from entering the building. Your experts will investigate the true case of the leak and provide a permanent repair solution.

## Low-ball Repair Offers & Band-Aid Repairs

Frequently, owners and owner associations inform a developer of a problem and the developer claims that a repair will be made. In fact, California's SB 800 (Civil Code Section 895) gives the developer a right to repair. For more on this, see Appendix C. Typically, a "low-ball" repair offer is then made and a "band-aid" repair is provided. Rather than expend the necessary money to get to the root of the problem, the developer would rather cover the cracks with stucco or paint over the stains. The reasons why those cracks or stains are happening in the first place are not addressed. Remember, you have the right to the home you thought you were buying and the one you were either implicitly or explicitly promised.

## Chapter Four Do's and Don'ts

## Do:

- Do review your CC&R's (Covenants, Conditions, and Restrictions) and ask the board or management if there is a question of whether you or your owner association are responsible for specific claims.
- Do be familiar with potential defects. Among the categories are: leaking windows, crooked floors, exterior stucco and siding cracks, im-

proper drainage, structural defects, improper material selection, faulty construction techniques, mold, and plumbing and electrical issues.

- Do maintain your property and mitigate damages.

## Don't:

- Don't just rely on the developer to define a defect or how to fix it.
- Don't let the developer make repairs unless you know the fix is permanent and responsible.
- Don't try to handle warranty claims yourself. The builder is better advised, trained, and financed.
- Don't let the developer make "Band-Aid" repairs. The defects will reappear next year.
- Don't trigger a statute of limitations problem by simply advising the developer of a defect.

# CHAPTER FIVE:
# THE RIGHT LAWYER AND EXPERTS

Effective coordination among owner association's board of directors, property managers, consultants, experts, and legal counsel is crucial to a successful defect case. Proving the existence of a defect is the task of retained experts. The lawyer assumes the responsibility of creating and maintaining these relationships on behalf of the client's best interest, and to protect the attorney-client privilege. In addition, construction defect lawsuits are among the most complex in the legal field. As a result, retaining the best possible legal counsel can make or break a case.

## Selecting the Right Law Firm

Should a defect arise in a single family home, the owners are responsible for finding an attorney to represent their interests. When a common interest development is experiencing common area construction defects, the association's board of directors decides whether to move forward with litigation with what law firm. In either case, the principles and methods employed are basically the same.

Where to begin is always a difficult first step. Trusted resources, such as property managers, may provide a recommendation or your own on-line research may guide the way. Law firms handling construction defect claims fall into two categories. First, are the law firms that limit its practice to construction defect pre-litigation and litigation claims. These firms have the experience and strength to work on a contingency fee model, advance costs on its line of credit, and are not paid until a case is concluded. Only a few of these firms practice solely in California while many are spread thin across various states. Second, are general practice law firms that may cover a wide array of legal issues from general corporate advise to owner association issues, such as CC&R enforcement. Construction defect litigation is only a small part of the expansive practice. These firms work mostly on an hourly or hybrid fee agreement, do not offer to advance costs, and require payment as you go through the litigation process.

Whomever you decide to interview, rate each firm on the basis of their reputation, knowledge of construction defect law, mediation experience, track record, settlement history, integrity, and whether the firm has the staying power to finance the lawsuit. Be upfront with your attorney regarding who will bring the action and who will be sued to avoid conflicts of interest. Legal counsel has an ethical responsibility to disclose any potential conflicts of interest in writing. For example, law firms that once represented developers or an owner's association general counsel who accepts a percentage of settlement fees awarded to a construction defect law firm, as well as the firm who provides the percentage to general counsel, would not be wise choices. There is no way to know how a lawyer's judgment will be affected by these dual allegiances.

Avoid hiring an attorney who is an owner or member of the association, or who has a close relationship with a board member. These types of close relationships may cloud a person's judgment. Neither should the association's general counsel be hired because of the need to remain impartial and provide a needed checks and balances. The association's counsel should be involved in hiring the most qualified defect lawyer on your behalf. They should never ask for or accept a fee sharing agreement from defect counsel in exchange for general counsel's referral.

Construction defect claims usually require many hours of work by attorneys, paralegals, and other support staff. Because of this, it is important to ensure that the firm you select is staffed to handle the work. A firm that is financially strong has more staying power and can finance the legal and expert costs associated with a defect claim. Interview the lawyer who will be running the case, and also the firm's senior attorney, especially for large, complex cases where owner associations are involved. For an attorney hiring criteria checklist and online resources, see Appendix A.

## Attorney-Client Privilege

Any communications between an attorney and client is privileged when the communication involves the underlying action or potential lawsuit. It is vital, therefore, that you, as a client, understand the sensitive nature of the information and not discuss the case with anyone except your attorney. You and your attorney should set up a procedure for communicating without divulging the information to a third party. Invoices or reports from retained consultants should be addressed to your attorney. In fact, a reasonable approach is to send all communications through your attorney. An effective method to protecting this privilege is to have counsel communicate with a designated board officer or litigation committee before each board meeting. The contact then can report to the board in an executive session. Of course, if you are a sole owner who is bringing suit, you should deal directly with the law firm.

## What the Attorney Does

In construction defect cases, the attorney is responsible for more than just recovering damages. His job also is to advise whether or not a claim exists in the first place. Competent and ethical attorneys will not take cases in which there is little to no chance of recovery. Contrary to popular myth, ethical attorneys do not want to put the time, effort, and money into a pointless lawsuit just to bill a client for fees.

The attorney must also make recommendations on commencing the pre-litigation and litigation claim process, retaining consultants and managing their time, finding developer insurance, alternative repair methods, hiring experienced contractors to assist with invasive testing, and the applicable statutes of limitations. Frequently, the attorney is asked to help finance the investigation and may also be requested to assess a settlement proposal that calls for developers to perform permanent repairs.

The attorney's role as advisor calls for understanding construction problems, solutions beyond court actions, and the after-trial process. In a construction defect case, the lawyer may represent a number of clients and is responsible to each. Most associations have general counsel to respond to questions association members may have regarding board member fiduciary responsibilities, financing, standing to sue, interpreting governing documents, updating association reserve studies and allocating association reserves, contracting consultants, settlement documents, and reconstruction. General counsel should also assist in selecting a law firm to represent its client for its construction defect claim, but should not also take on this role, nor should general counsel ask for or accept a percentage of a recovery from defect counsel.

Tasks your defect law firm should perform include:

- Initial due diligence and fiduciary duty case review. This is the first task your attorney will undertake. It includes:
- An onsite preliminary inspection by consultants and experts to determine the existence of any defects.
- A meeting with the association's Board of Directors, management company, or individual owners, when applicable, to discuss legal options.
- A survey of all owners to determine the extent and scope of the defects, and a full report.
- A preliminary review of all documents and files to prepare a statute of limitations analysis.
- Conducting site visits with select independent experts to verify existing common-area problems and consumer complaints.
- Developing a preliminary budget regarding expert investigations.
- Meeting again with the client to discuss findings and recommendations.
- Attend important board meetings as required or requested.
- Send monthly status letters.
- Send a monthly accounting of expenses.
- Update owners or association board of directors on new state regulations and case law.
- Assist in locating reconstruction experts and provide findings and recommendations after a settlement or verdict.
- Estimate financial expenditures.
- Attend annual owner association meetings as is required or requested and update members with quarterly status letters.
- Help find financing for necessary repairs that must be undertaken before settlement or judgment.

## What's It Going to Cost?

The consumer will make the decision as to which firm to hire and under what type of agreement. In most jurisdictions, a fee agreement must comply with state bar rules, local statutes, and court rules. These laws and rules typically require that all agreements be in writing, that the client be provided with a copy of the agreement, and that the client be notified that the fees are negotiable. If the attorney fails to meet the mandatory requirements, the client can rescind the agreement.

Typically, these agreements come in one of three following options: contingency, hourly, or hybrid.

- **Contingency Fee Agreement.** This means the attorney receives a percentage of any recovery only upon a successful recover and, at a minimum, should advance all litigation and retained expert costs. According to Consumer Attorneys of California (CAOC), 25% to 40% is considered fair and reasonable and contingent agreements promote efficiency while helping to prevent frivolous lawsuits. For more on this, See Appendix A. This type of agreement should always transfer the economic burden of litigation away from the client and to the attorney. Only a few law firms with a larger line of credit can offer this.

- **Hourly Fee Agreement.** This means the fee is a fixed per hour rate for the time a lawyer spends on the matter. This can range from $225-$500 or more per hour. When an hourly agreement is selected, the association will be required to pay its law firm, litigation expenses, and retained expert fees each month. Law firms working under an hourly fee agreement covers its overhead and profits with monthly billing and does not share in the financial burdens of litigation. The entire risk of a successful construction defect is places on the client. Should you decide to go with an hourly fee agreement, do not hesitate to ask your attorney for a budget of their time and costs before every step of the process. It is every lawyer's dream to work by the hour and receive payment without regard to the outcome of the case.

- **Hybrid Agreement.** This combines contingent and hourly fees by lowering each rate and adjusting what needs to be paid and when. A typical hybrid agreement may come in one of two ways. First, hourly fees are reduced by 50% and the contingency fee is kept at 20% to 25%. Second, a firm will start on an hourly fee and then switch to a contingent fee after certain point. Some law firms sell their hourly agreement, tout it as a more cost effective way of litigating, knowing full well that at some point the financial burdens will overwhelm the client and a switch to a contingency will have to occur. In any one of these scenarios, the hourly fees are due each month but such agreements may differ when it comes to advancing expert costs. When a law firm does not share such costs, the hybrid becomes the best of both worlds for the law firm. Litigation and expert costs burden the client, while the law firm covers its operating expense on an ongoing basis, and, upon final settlement, receives a percentage of the recovery.

Problems can occur when the responsible party agrees to repair the property instead of making cash payments or a developer agrees to buy back the property. In those situations, who pays the attorney and experts? When this occurs, your attorney should negotiate fees and expert costs separately so the owner association is made whole. If that fails, the association board should prioritize repairs and fix the major problems causing life safety issues and ongoing property damage. Such agreements should include language stating that reasonable attorney fees will be paid to your lawyer. In a buy-back situation, the agreement should base the fees on the reasonable value of the property that is repurchased. The agreement should also include a provision for arbitration or mediation should a dispute arise regarding repairs.

## Changing Attorneys Mid-Stream

The client always has the absolute legal right to fire an attorney and retain another. When the client does fire the attorney, however, the lawyer is entitled to "reasonable fees" for his work because it is hardly fair to have one lawyer spend what could be months to work up a case, only to have another step in and take the fees. Under a contingency agreement, these fees for the first lawyer will come out of any settlement or judgment eventually achieved. If hourly, fees will be due in the normal payment cycle at the time of settlement or resolution. Another reason not to go hourly. In contingency fee cases, the attorney waits for a portion of the settlement or judgment. When changing lawyers, you can negotiate with your new lawyer to pay directly the reasonable costs and fees of your previous lawyer. The replaced lawyer can file a lien but only on the fees that the case brings upon resolution, not a lien on the person or property of an owner or owner association.

It is never too late to make changes and don't ever think you are in too deep. Getting another attorney's opinion should be free and would give you greater insight into your case at the very least. Lawyers often have very different ways of viewing a case. Many clients run out of money with hourly lawyers and feel there is no way out but to give up or give in for less than a case is worth. That is also a good time to talk to a firm that will take your case on contingency.

## Chapter Five Do's and Don'ts

### Do:

- Do meet with a couple of law firms and obtain separate proposals from each.
- Do evaluate and review a law firm's knowledge and experience with construction defect cases, their trial and mediation experience, track record, settlement history, reputation, integrity, fees, and ability to advance expert and litigation costs.
- Do tell your attorney of all potential plaintiffs and defendants so he or she can check for conflicts of interest.
- Do check references.
- Do check to see if the potential law firm has the staff, resources, and finances to effectively pursue the claim.
- Do establish a protocol to efficiently communicate with your attorney and maintain confidentiality.
- Do negotiate fees.

Do get an estimate of fees up front and then have it updated quarterly if you hire an attorney on an hourly fee basis.

### Don't:

- Don't hesitate to have a second attorney give an opinion, even if your attorney has already made a claim or filed suit. The opinion should be free of charge.
- Don't hire an attorney who is an owner in the development or is an association board member.

## HOME AND CONDO DEFECTS

- Don't hire the association's corporate or general counsel law firm to pursue a construction defect claim. Conflicts exist. You need separation and accountability.
- Don't hire an attorney just because he or she has a close relationship with a board member.
- Don't limit yourself by your first choice of attorneys; if you are not satisfied with your current attorney, you have the right to change at any time.

# CHAPTER SIX:
# FINANCING THE LAWSUIT

Financing a construction defect claim can be costly for high-rise condominiums as well as single-family homes. Experts and other professionals, through the guidance of your counsel, work to find a solution to your problems. Unforeseen costs, such as repairs during litigation and relocation expenses forced on a client by health hazards or any other array of issues that may make a house or condo unlivable, can add up. To throw fuel to the fire, unchecked developers and their insurance companies are also well funded and can drive up your litigation costs.

## Raising the Money

A discussion about how best to finance the litigation needs to take place early on in the process. Possible sources are:

- **Litigation counsel**. Only select law firms with enough experience in construction defects can finance costs with their line of credit. This may be the only way for a single-family owner and the best way for an owner association to pay these costs. These costs can be forgiven if there is no settlement or other recovery sufficient to cover them.

- **Association reserves**. The law in California allows the use of common interest association reserve funds to pursue claims related to property repair, restoration, replacement, or maintenance. Reserve funds also may be transferred to general operating accounts to meet short-term cash flow problems. Of course, the transferred funds must be returned to the reserve fund, usually within a set time period unless the association extends the time limits.

- **Loans**. Associations can borrow money, but there are inherent problems in this challenging economy. Certain lending institutions will make loans to associations in good standing and with low delinquencies and high owner occupancy. Defect counsel and an association's general counsel should be familiar with these lenders. A good option for the individual owner bringing a claim is to go to the original lender on their mortgage, who will be interested in maintaining the value of the home because it is the collateral for the original loan.

- **Special assessments**. Many association CC&R's require a vote to pass a special assessment because raising dues is usually limited to increments of five percent at a time. Passing a special assessment can be an alternative method of financing litigation costs, but these assessments are not very popular with owners.

## Is the Developer Able to Pay?

Before proceeding with the investigation of the claim and hiring experts, experienced counsel should make sure the developer or any other potential defendant has the resources to pay a settlement or judgment. Even if the developer or other defendants are no longer in business, there should be insurance available to satisfy a judgment. It makes little sense to expend the time, effort, and expense of a lawsuit if it is impossible to collect.

Also, your attorney should explain the construction defect claim process. He or she will investigate every member of the developer's team and will want access to all of the information in your files, such as brochures, warrantees, sales information, or governmental filings. Allowing your lawyer full access to everything in your files will aid in the preparation and pursuit of your claim, including discovering potential defendants. Developers often form limited liability corporations (LLC) to build homes, and then, when the homes are completed, collapse the corporation. After the developer collapses the LLC, tracking the responsible entity or person is more difficult.

Skilled counsel may be able to circumvent the need for prolonged litigation. Insurance companies and developers usually know the top construction defect lawyers. After evaluating the case, and your attorney's reputation, insurance companies may decide to cut their losses and settle the case though early mediation efforts. This is especially true when the experts and consultants your attorney hired have conducted an effective investigation, thus allowing your attorney the ability to present a persuasive case for damages. Not only should you question your attorney about previous trial results, but also about early mediation and settlement results. Only about five percent of cases ever go to trial.

## Chapter Six Do's and Don'ts

### Do:

- Do have your attorney explore the ability of the developer's insurance coverage to pay a claim early in the construction defect claims process.
- Do have your attorney explain the various methods of financing a lawsuit.
- Do explore early settlement options with counsel.

### Don't:

- Don't proceed without carefully analyzing all pre-litigation and litigation costs.

# CHAPTER SEVEN:
# WHO CAN SUE?

Historically, only the property owner who bought property directly from a developer had the right to legal redress. The original buyer was said to have "privity," a direct contract relationship, with the developer. Therefore, with the right to the property's possession, the original purchaser was said to be the "real party in interest." Over time, the law developed to allow both owner associations and subsequent buyers to bring suit.

Problems can still arise in determining who gets to recover if the property changes hands during litigation. Is it the person who owned the property at the beginning of the action, or is it the person who owned the property when the case was completed?

In California, the general rule is the person whose interest is injured from the defect is the person who has the right to the lawsuit recovery. Determining whose interest is injured can become very complex, and depends on the facts of each situation. For example, someone who owned property at the beginning of a lawsuit and sold the property during the middle of litigation, but received less than full value of the property because of the claim, has the right to compensation. Or these rights can be assigned to the buyer. Conversely, someone who sold the property for full value has no such rights.

The moral of the story is this: If you sell property during an action, you must disclose that the property is involved in litigation and you should, through your broker, real estate agent, or lawyer, discuss and agree with the buyer which party has the right to recover. The results of this discussion should be put into writing and included in your sales contract. The California Legislature in SB 800 (Civil Code Section 895) allows subsequent buyers the same rights as the original buyer. For more on this, see Appendix C.

## Can an Owner Association's Board of Directors Bring Suit?

In California, the number of common interest developments is increasing each year and include high-rise, luxury condominiums, town-homes, stock cooperatives, or single-family residences. These are defined as "non-profit mutual benefit associations created for the purpose of managing a common interest development." Typically, an owner association acts on behalf of its membership through a board of directors. When problems arise, the association's board of directors can bring an action for faulty construction. But, what they can sue for depends on how the property involved is owned. What this means depends on the type of project and the responsibilities that are defined in a set of CC&R's.

When a private buyer purchases a home built on separate lots, the owner is responsible for his or her own property, and the association's common areas are streets, sidewalks, or recreation areas, such as a community pool. In condominium projects, the association owns the walls and other structures, from the roof down to the garage. Owners, on the other hand, own only their "air-space", which is the internal walls, plumbing inside the unit, carpeting or hardwood floors, mechanical ducts and vents that serve only that one unit, and fixtures. In any event, the owner is responsible to bring his or her own action against the developer for defects that affect their space. In California, under Civil Code Section 1368.3, the association's board of directors has the right and obligation to bring common area construction defect claims on behalf of the entire membership.

In most states, if the potential exists for a lawsuit to be brought by the owner association, the board of directors has a duty to investigate the situation and, if a defect exits, bring the lawsuit. A board's failure to bring the claim in a timely manner will ultimately shift this burden to the association membership, who, through large assessments, will have to make these repairs. The prior board and its members may then be held liable. While it is important that the association have "directors and officers" insurance coverage, newer policies have excluded coverage for board members who fail to act responsibly or heed advice of professionals (lawyers, property managers, or other management consultants) when faced with construction defect decisions.

Before deciding who can be plaintiffs, your lawyer must carefully examine all pertinent documents and recordings.

## Class Action

Class action lawsuits allow large numbers of "similarly situated" owners to bring a claim as one unit. Generally, this is a preferred method for single-family housing developments without an association. For example, if a developer built a group of single-family homes in a development with substandard roofing that results in leaks, all affected homeowners may be considered similarly situated and can join together to litigate as a class.

Before moving forward, the "class" must be certified by the court as proper, which can be a fairly complex procedure. One person, who should be one of the original owners, is the named plaintiff and is chosen to be the "class representative". Courts look for common facts and apply certain standards when considering whether to certify a group of plaintiffs as a class. The courts also tend to vary radically on who they will certify as a class. Also know that developers fight certification to limit the number of potential claimants. Developers and their attorneys understand that owners' interests vary, and if alone, many will not bring a claim forward out of embarrassment, apathy, fear of disclosure, or of the need to sell or refinance.

Even when a court will not certify a class, individual owners may still be required to join together in the same lawsuit against a developer. Courts prefer to resolve a set of common circumstances among the similar parties at one time.

In addition, courts generally require attorneys to meet certain qualifications before the court will allow them to be lead counsel representing the plaintiffs in class action lawsuits. If a court certifies the class and the attorney meets the qualifications to represent the class, individual class members may "opt out" of the class and bring their claims separately.

Attorney fees and costs are frequently handled differently in class action lawsuits than in individual lawsuits. In some jurisdictions, the losing party can be required to pay the prevailing party's attorney fees and other costs. In other jurisdictions, the plaintiffs will be liable individually for the defendant's fees and costs if the plaintiffs fail to prevail. Prudent clients will require that their attorneys carefully and completely explain these possibilities.

## Chapter Seven Do's and Don'ts:

### Do:

- Do carefully explain to potential buyers if you are in the middle of a defect dispute, and who will receive any recovery. Put such information in the purchase agreement because you can assign your rights.
- Do have your attorney decide if the owner association's board of directors, individual owners, or both should bring suit.
- Do understand that an owner association is a term used in many different common interest development entities, such as, low-, mid-, and high-rise condominiums, townhomes, or single-family housing developments; and generally the owner association owns and maintains the common areas.
- Do have your attorney explain what the individual owners own and what the owner association must maintain and repair under the CC&R's.

### Don't:

- Don't fail to carefully explain to prospective buyers if you are in the middle of a defect dispute and who will receive any recovery. Put such information in the purchase agreement. Consider assigning your rights if you own a home.

# CHAPTER EIGHT: STEPS BEFORE THE DANCE CAN BEGIN

A competent attorney's goal is to explore options for settlement with the developer's insurance defense attorney before litigation begins because an early resolution that responsibly repairs the defective conditions saves money for everyone involved. As a result and at the request of the insurance and building industry, with opposition from consumer groups, many states across the nation have passed laws to encourage pre-litigation resolution.

California has two controlling statues relating to pre-litigation steps, one is called The Calderon Process (Civil Code Section 1375 et seq.) and the other is referred to as SB 800 (Civil Code Section 895 et seq.). A third pre-litigation procedure can come from your developer, who opts out of the statutory framework by drafting its own pre-litigation steps in the CC&R's. The purpose of any one of these is to provide an opportunity for early settlement by notifying the developer of a defect, who then has a right to inspect the property and make offers to repair or settle.

What sounds simple is actually a complex set of rules and regulations that are full of pitfalls for the uninitiated. Your attorney must have the experience to properly guide you step by step though the pre-litigation process. Your attorney should know which process you are to follow or whether you are exempt and can immediately file your lawsuit, who you are to notify and how, what time limits and deadlines are to be met, what type of inspections should take place, or whether the developer's offer to repair or settle is adequate. Only after these pre-litigation steps have correctly been extinguished can an owner or owner association file a lawsuit against the developer.

To get an understanding of what goes into these pre-litigation steps, see the attached flow chart for the SB 800 below (Civil Code Section 895 et seq. see Appendix C). You may also visit www.constructiondefects.com, where we further discuss both the Calderon Process and SB 800.

# Sample SB 800 Timeline for Pre-Litigation Procedures

| Day 1 | Association's written notice of violation served on builder |
|---|---|

↓

| Day 14 | Written acknowledgement of association's notice due from builder (14 days from notice) |
|---|---|

↓

| Day 28 | Builder to have completed initial inspection of building (14 days after acknowledgement) |
|---|---|

↓

| Day 44 | Builder sends HOA documents, plans, specs, grading plans, final soil reports, DRE reports, engineering calculations (30 days after request to inspect) |
|---|---|

↓

## AFTER INITIAL INSPECTION, BUILDER MAY...

↓                    ↓

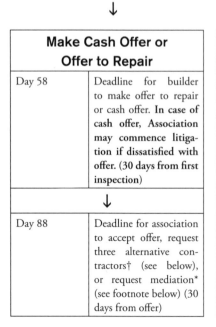

### Make Cash Offer or Offer to Repair

| Day 58 | Deadline for builder to make offer to repair or cash offer. **In case of cash offer, Association may commence litigation if dissatisfied with offer.** (30 days from first inspection) |
|---|---|

↓

| Day 88 | Deadline for association to accept offer, request three alternative contractors† (see below), or request mediation* (see footnote below) (30 days from offer) |
|---|---|

### Request Second Inspection

| Day 31 | Deadline for builder to request optional second inspection of building (3 days from initial inspection) |
|---|---|

↓

| Day 68 | Builder to have completed second inspection of building (40 days from initial inspection) |
|---|---|

| | | | |
|---|---|---|---|
| Day 102 | Builder to have scheduled repair work to begin based on mutually acceptable dates. (14 days from acceptance of offer) If no permit has been obtained, deadline is extended until 5 days after permit is obtained. | Day 98 | Deadline for builder to make offer to repair or cash offer. **In case of cash offer, Association may commence litigation if dissatisfied with offer. (30 days from second inspection)** |
| | ↓ | | ↓ |
| Day 222 | Date by which builder is to make "every effort" to have repairs completed (120 days) | Day 128 | Deadline for association to accept offer & authorize repair, request three alternative contractors† (see below), or request mediation* (see footnote below) (30 days from offer) |
| | | | ↓ |
| | | Day 142 | Builder to have scheduled repair work to begin based on mutually acceptable dates. (14 days from acceptance of offer) If no permit has been obtained, deadline is extended until 5 days after permit is obtained. |
| | ↓ | | ↓ |

| | |
|---|---|
| After repairs completed | Before action may be filed, association must request mediation if no mediation has yet taken place |
| Within 15 days of request for mediation | Mediation must be completed |
| After unsuccessful conclusion of mediation | Court action may be filed |

† If Association Requests That Builder Provide Alternative Contractors

| Where Builder Has Made Offer After Single Inspection | | Where Builder Has Requested Second Inspection | |
|---|---|---|---|
| Day 108 | Deadline for builder to have alternative contractors inspect building. (20 days from request for alternative contractor) | Day 148 | Deadline for builder to have alternative contractors inspect building (20 days from request for alternative contractors) |
| ↓ | | ↓ | |
| Day 143 | Deadline for builder to provide names of alternative contractors (35 days after request) | Day 163 | Deadline for builder to present names of alternative contractors and offer to repair (35 days after request for alternative contractors). Must be accompanied by an offer to mediate. |
| ↓ | | ↓ | |
| Day 163 | Deadline for association to accept offer or request mediation* (20 days after presentation of contractors) | Day 183 | **Deadline for association to authorize alternative contractors to perform repairs. (20 days after presentation of contractors).** |
| ↓ | | ↓ | |
| Day 177 | Builder to have scheduled repair work to begin based on mutually acceptable dates. (14 days from selection). If no permit has been obtained before, deadline is extended until five days after permit is obtained | Day 197 | Builder to have scheduled repair work to begin based on mutually acceptable dates. (14 days from acceptance/selection of contractors) If no permit has been obtained, deadline is extended until five days after permit is obtained. |
| ↓ | | ↓ | |
| Day 297 | Date by which builder is to make "every effort" to have repairs completed. (120 days from commencement of repairs) | Day 317 | Date by which builder is to make "every effort" to have repairs completed. (120 days from commencement of repairs) |

| ↓ | ↓ |
|---|---|
| After repairs completed | Before action may be filed, association must request mediation if no mediation has yet taken place |
| Within 15 days of request for mediation | Mediation must be completed |
| After unsuccessful conclusion of mediation | Court action may be filed |

\* If the association requests mediation at any point before repair is complete, the parties have 15 days from the date of the request to mediate the case. (Civil Code § 919.) If successful, the builder must, within seven days of completion of the mediation, schedule the repairs to commence, thus commencing the 120-day period for performing the repairs. (Civil Code § 921.)

If mediation is unsuccessful, the association may initiate a court action.

## Reasons why these time periods may be extended under SB 800:

- Builder requests to commence contractual procedures outside SB 800 (Civil Code 914)
- Commencement of repairs subject to:
  - Availability of association/owners
  - Builder's contractor or alternative contractor
  - Mediation
  - When building permit is issued; builder to act diligently
- Builder's desire to fix only part of defects/building standards violations identified. (Civil Code 924)
- Agreement of parties to extend time limits. (Civil Code 930)
- If new claims are subsequently discovered, unless related to the same violated building standards in the current claim, a new SB 800 process has to start (unless builder stipulates)

## Tolling of Statutes:

- If applicable statutes of limitations have otherwise run, the time period for filing a complaint is extended by:
  - 100 days after repair is completed or 45 days after the time for responding to the notice of claim has expired

Pre-litigation steps can take months and most claims will not settle during this time because of the complexity of the issues and the real costs to make responsible repairs will come out of pocket from the developer until insurance is triggered at the filing of the claim. A skilled construction defect law firm will best understand how to use this time wisely. Negotiating a Case Management/Pretrial Order when it becomes apparent that the filing of a claim is imminent and having a complaint ready to be filed when necessary are steps that can be taken to efficiently keep your process moving forward into litigation.

## Chapter Eight Do's and Don'ts

### Do:

- Do promptly provide any information your lawyer needs to complete pre-litigation steps required by law.
- Do familiarize yourself with whatever pre-litigation steps your jurisdiction may have.
- Do act promptly. Many states have complex time limits on pre-litigation steps. Some require action one or two years after the property is completed.

### Don't:

- Don't procrastinate in doing what your attorney has asked.
- Don't act slowly. You must meet the deadlines, or you could lose your right to your claim.
- Don't believe the builder has your interests in mind. Remember, they caused the problem and must pay to fix all deficiencies.
- Don't try to do this yourself. You are bound to make a mistake.

# CHAPTER NINE: WHAT LAWYERS ARGUE TO COLLECT

Construction defect law developed from centuries established legal theories and are continually influenced by a myriad set of state statutes that can be, even for the most skilled attorney, difficult to understand. We have written several legal textbooks that explain these issues to lawyers, judges, and mediators, and stay on top of updates and changes in the law with yearly supplements. A competent lawyer should have access to a library of information and an understanding that law is always in a state of flux. Knowledge of and staying current with the law are essential tools to skillfully prosecute a construction defect case.

Gaining a basic understanding of the legal theories and principles will help you stay engaged and understand what the attorneys are saying. One such area is the type of actions your attorney will bring against the developer. Rather than list every legal dart a lawyer has in his quiver, we decided to focus on legal theories most commonly used in the construction defect claims process.

## Strict Liability

Under a theory of strict liability, one need not prove anyone was at fault. An owner or owner association only needs to show that damage exists and the developer is responsible. The argument behind strict liability is that consumers can seldom be expected to know as much about mass marketed and mass produced, technologically sophisticated housing products as the developer and manufacturer.

For example, when a home buyer flips a light switch he or she cannot be expected to understand the relationship of current to voltage (the two are inversely proportional and total power equals voltage times amperage, or $P=I \times E$), or which wiring types work the best and last the longest (gold and platinum, but copper is the best substitute), or what wiring diameter is required to carry a certain load (depends on voltage, current, and type of wiring), or the size of an electron, or whether parallel or series circuitry works the best in homes (generally parallel), or the atomic theory behind nuclear power and quark theory (beats us, but it has something to do with spin and *Finnegan's Wake*). One shouldn't even be required to know the difference between direct current, DC, or alternating current, AC. DC goes directly between positive and negative, while AC shifts polarity in a sine wave according to its frequency. Household currency is AC, 120 volts, and shifts 60 times a second.

What one needs to know is that when one flips the switch, the light fixture is supposed to produce light. If it doesn't, and the light bulb isn't burnt out, and the lamp is plugged in, there could be a defect. In California, all defects, whether involving electrical, plumbing, water intrusion, drainage, structural deficiencies, or framing, have been listed in SB 800 (Civil Code Section 895 et seq.) For more on this, see Appendix C. Failing to meet any of the building standards permits a claim to be made whether in strict liability, negligence, breach of implied warranty, or simply of an SB 800 statutory violation.

Besides not having to show fault, another advantage of SB 800 statutory violation or strict liability claims is that one need not be the original buyer who made the contract with the developer (in legalese this is called "being in privity" with the developer). One can be the third, forth, or fifth buyer and still bring suit so long as it is done within a statutory time limit. The ability of a subsequent home purchaser to make a construction defect claim is very important. We live in an increasingly mobile society and it is not unusual for people to move their households every few years.

Frequently, however, defects do not immediately manifest themselves. For example, a home in a climate with little rain will not leak until there is a moderate amount of rain. The result is that window or roof defects could take several years to become apparent. Another example is a beam or joist that is cracked when installed. It may take several years for the beam or joist to fail and cause structural damage.

Strict liability requires only that the house, condominium, or manufactured component such as window or furnace, is defective and that the defect causes damage. Refer to California's SB 800, Sections 896 and 897, for specific building standard violations. For more on this, see Appendix C. The defect can be in design, site selection, engineering, workmanship, materials, construction technique, or a plethora of other things. The most frequent cause of a defect is a home not built in accord with the approved plans and specifications, industry design standards, or building code requirements. But under strict liability or SB 800 there is no need to identify which designer, engineer, or contractor was in error. One need simply prove a defect exists.

### Breach of Implied Warranty

The implied warranty of merchantability was the first intrusion into the old doctrine of *caveat emptor*. "Implied" means the warranty is not written nor otherwise expressed. Basically, it means when one buys a home, it is implied the house should be habitable. For example, a buyer reasonably expects the lights to work, the roof to keep water out, and the house not to fall down a hill.

The "breach of implied warranty" legal theory is used in those states that have not attached strict liability, when the statute of limitations has expired, or when the house was not a mass-produced consumer item. California has extended implied warranty to later purchasers, subject to the statute of limitations.

### Breach of Express Warranty

Many developers include written, express warranties within sales contracts. This is similar to a warranty one receives on an automobile. As with a car, an express warranty is enforceable only by the original purchaser unless the warranty states otherwise.

Note that, simply because a purchasing agreement states you have a two year warranty or guarantee does not mean you are limited to that number of years. Some homebuyers will discover a defect, then read the purchase agreement that says they only have a one or two year warranty. They will assume the warranty has expired and not pursue the claim. This could be disastrous. Again, notify an attorney and your owner association if you suspect a construction defect.

## Violation of SB 800 Standards; Negligence Per Se

With SB 800 (Civil Code Section 895) the California legislature gives consumers some clarity. It allows consumers to show the builder violated on one or more of the standards of construction laid out in Sections 896 and 897 and by doing so shifts the entire burden of proof over to the builder to show he met those standards. This is a very powerful tool to use in construction defect claim. For more on this, see Appendix C.

## Negligence

As discussed previously, negligence requires one to show the developer had a duty to build in a reasonable manner and breached that duty, causing damages. For example, a developer has a duty to use undamaged lumber. If the developer uses a cracked beam, and as a result the house collapses, the developer is probably negligent. In addition, if a developer or builder negligently hired or supervised a subcontractor, the developer can be found liable in negligence.

Negligence is often unnecessary against developers in states that have adopted strict liability causes of action. However, because many service professionals such as architects and engineers, brokers, property managers, and real estate agents cannot be sued in strict liability (because they do not mass produce a product), negligence still is an effective cause of action.

Also, if the developer was the seller and broker, the developer can be held liable in negligence for failing to disclose building problems, such as known or suspected defects discovered before the sale. Plus, if the developer sits as a member of an owner association's board of directors -- which in early development phases he usually does -- and fails to perform a duty as a board member, such as filing a claim for construction defects against himself or underfunding association reserves, he may be liable for negligence under the association's CC&R's.

## Fraud, Deceit, and Misrepresentation

Lawyers and legal scholars can spend lifetimes and millions of words distinguishing actual fraud from constructive fraud, and constructive fraud from intentional misrepresentation or deceit. Each has a highly technical meaning that means little to anyone except lawyers. Also, various statutes in various states provide various definitions for the same terms. To save you the time, money, and effort of attending law school, studying for the Bar Exam, and hopefully passing it, we will provide very general and truncated definitions.

As a very general rule, each of the three is an omission of a known fact, or the statement as fact of something not true, that is relied upon and causes damages. For example, you purchase a home built atop a toxic dump or near a landslide and the seller knows the condition exists but either lies to you or fails to tell you. You rely upon these statements or omissions, and after you buy the home you cannot resell the property. You have been a victim of at least one of the items in this category. The important thing is that you tell your lawyer everything you can think of about your injury so he or she can decide if a fraud, deceit, or misrepresentation has occurred.

**Caution**: Fraud or intentional misrepresentation triggers no insurance coverage because insurance policies generally exclude intentional acts. And to prove fraud requires a higher standard of proof, that of clear and convincing evidence. If you believe the builder mislead you, consider asserting a claim for negligent misrepresentation or gross negligence.

### Nuisance

Nuisance occurs when something is injurious to health, indecent, offensive to the senses, an obstruction to the enjoyment of life or property, or obstructs the free passage or use of a public right of way such as a lake, river, creek, street, or park.

The advantage of a nuisance theory is that it is a continuing tort, which means that as long as the nuisance exists, the time period for filing a complaint never runs out. For example, if on your twenty-fifth birthday you buy a new house that has an offensive odor, and that odor continues to smell, that possibly would be considered a continuing tort. If the odor continues for fifty years, you still might be able to bring a lawsuit on your seventy-fifth birthday.

Of course, this is an extreme example, and it is doubtful courts would allow it, but courts do not like disallowing a valid claim just because one was a little late filing a complaint, and lawyers are always searching for ways to encourage judges to give people their day in court.

## Multiple Causes of Action

Almost always, an attorney will allege more than one cause of action in a complaint. For example, an attorney may claim on behalf of their client that the developer and others are liable in fraud, negligence, strict liability and negligence per se, a violation of statutory building standards like the California SB 800 (Civil Code Section 895), nuisance, and violation of an implied warranty, then ask for compensatory and punitive damages (if permitted in the jurisdiction).

Attorneys allege more than one cause of action for several reasons. First, some defendants may be liable for different behaviors in different causes of actions. Second, there may be a statute of limitations problem that the attorney is deftly attempting to circumvent. Or, just because a developer is liable under strict liability, doesn't mean it isn't a good idea to show the judge and jury how the developer was negligent and how what he or she did wrong caused your damages. With the additions of statutory standards like the California SB 800 (Civil Code Section 895), there is a powerful cause of action for a violation of the statute. Once you show the violation, for example, cracked stucco, leaks from windows or roofs, or faulty drainage, just to name a few, the burden to prove the case shifts to the builder and developer to show that they met the standard, and this can be a very difficult task. This will give your case more force. In addition, in a very few causes of action, attorneys' fees are available where otherwise they might not.

## Chapter Nine Do's and Don'ts
### Do:

- Do try to learn some of the important terminology that applies to your case, for example, defects, statute of limitations, conflicts of interest, or contingency fees.

### Don't:

- Don't be embarrassed to ask your lawyer questions if you don't understand something about your case.

# CHAPTER TEN: INSURANCE

When buying a house, there is a stack of papers waiting to be signed. It is very unlikely that a buyer will step away from the emotions present at the point of signing to ask the sales agent about the developer's construction defect insurance coverage. Whether or not the developer and other defendants have insurance to cover defects in residential construction is an issue of utmost importance.

Insurance companies and developers know defect cases can be expensive, resulting in considerable losses. When a claim arises, the developer's insurance company will reach into their stable of attorneys to analyze any policy and insurance law in an attempt to avoid coverage or spread their losses out to general and subcontracting insurance policies. To better prepare for your claim, your attorney should review a copy of the developer's insurance policies as early on in the construction defect claims process as possible. Your attorney needs to understand the coverages and policy exclusions and limitations, and discover the most appropriate means of correctly tapping into the developer's coverage because it often determines the overall strategy.

The policy coverage available quite literally can make the difference between a great result and a terrible outcome. Often, a developer either has no assets, or assets that are insufficient to cover damages. Commonly, the corporation under which the developer did business, is a Limited Liability Company (LLC) that has been dissolved or has distributed all its profits from this development. Insurance for the developer, builder, and subcontractors is the only viable source of recovery for owners and owner associations.

We cannot stress enough the importance of not overlooking one of the most essential tasks of your attorney, which is to evaluate the available insurance early and often. In California, unlike some states, the laws allow coverage for construction defects. The following discussion provides a framework for understanding insurance and how it affects your claim.

## Third-Party Claims

Third-party claims are the nucleus of most construction defect cases. When an owner association sues a developer, the developer will pass the lawsuit to his insurance company, making the owner association the third-party claimant. This, of course, assumes the developer, architect, contractor, or sub-contractor has insurance. Most of the involved parties do, because in states like California, any of these entities would have a tough time doing business without insurance coverage. The real question becomes how much insurance coverage is available and whether you will get to this insurance before any other real or potential claimants. Policy exclusions also play a huge role in this analysis. Insurance companies continue to add exclusions, diminishing the amount of coverage available.

## Coverage: The Big Question

As has already been stated, the big question, and often a multi-million dollar one, is whether adequate insurance is available to cover the damages caused by the defects to your home or condo. Insurance is big business, and as such, insurance companies are beholden to the bottom line. These companies want to collect premiums, and minimize claims payments. Another way to put it, by collecting more, and paying out less, insurance companies make bigger profits for their Wall Street investors.

As a result, when arguing against a construction defect claim, insurance companies generally take the following defensive positions. The insurance company will assert that damages do not exist. Where damages are shown to exist, the insurance company will try to argue that the damages are not their client's (the developer) fault and therefore not the insurance company's responsibility to pay the claim. The insurance company may also simply argue that an insurance policy has an exclusion that applies to the damages in question. This can all be frustrating to a consumer who simply wants to have the problem fixed.

Developers usually receive coverage from the following sources: their own policies, policies of the general and sub-contractors they hire, or through a "wrap policy". A wrap policy places all of the contractors involved in a project under the same insurance policy. When any of these policy sources are emptied, they may have excess or umbrella coverage or the general and subcontractors may have their own policies.

Successfully pursuing third-party claims requires your attorney to analyze numerous factors. First, he or she must understand the standard comprehensive general liability policy and what it usually includes, and its endorsements. For example, if a wrap policy is not large enough or covers more than one project built by a developer, it may not provide sufficient coverage for your association's claim. Moreover, a policy may have a large "deductible" (called in the industry a self insured retention, or SIR) that a developer must pay before an insurance company will step in to defend a claim. Recently, these have been seen as high as $500,000 to $1,000,000. And, don't forget, there may be insurance to cover that deductible. Secondly, he or she must understand the responsibilities among successive holders, excess, and umbrella insurance policies (a developer may have up to $1 million with one carrier and $1-2 million with another). Third, your attorney must know what constitutes an "occurrence" (most policies say they will cover only so much money "per occurrence"), and lastly, what is and is not covered by the policy. In one recent case, the general contractor's insurance company served a twelve-page letter denying coverage for an owner association's claim based on a residential exclusion in the policy. This exclusion applies where a contractor is involved in a residential (home or condos) project. And even thought the broker know about the work the contractor was doing, failed to remove that exclusion.

When choosing a construction defect firm, ask if the attorneys have either have done insurance coverage work, and how they expect to evaluate complex coverage issues as they arise. Some attorneys have even worked for insurance companies in the past. This background is invaluable because it is a sign that an attorney understands insurance coverage issues and how insurance companies operate.

Be wary of a firm who acts as general counsel to owner associations when a defect claim arises. Typically, these firms have limited defect claims experience or insurance knowledge, and charge by the hour. A lack of experience will cost the association time and money. It is common knowledge that these law firms do the general counsel work daily to get first shot at any defect claims for which they can bill more hourly time. Most experienced defect counsel are willing to take a risk and finance the case from the start and not deplete the HOA reserves or require the HOA to obtain bank financing.

## Reservation of Rights

When a claim is sent to a developer's insurance company, the company usually will issue what is called a "reservation of rights." This means the insurance company will investigate the claim, defend the developer in a lawsuit, but reserves the right to reject the claim or refuse to pay a settlement or verdict.

Some factors used by insurance companies to determine their liabilities are whether the policies limit or exclude coverage for the types of incidents involved in a claim and whether an incident involved in a claim may not have occurred while the policy was in effect. Information on how a claim fits into a policy's limitations may not be available until after a claim is investigated and defended. Sometimes, part of a claim is covered and another is not. Frequently, investigations can lead an insurance company to file a lawsuit against another insurance company or against its own insured, asking the court to determine its rights. A carrier may decide it has no liability, and thus, no responsibility to defend a claim. When this occurs, the company will seek to be reimbursed for defense costs.

To add to these complexities, the owner or owner association bringing a construction defect claim never receives a reservation of rights letter. However, reservation of rights issues can influence how a case should be brought. For example, few policies cover anything other than claims for property damage. So, claims for defects that show no resulting property damage will be denied. Therefore, experienced counsel must be careful how they draft the original complaint so that the insurance carrier will not deny the claim outright.

Just because a jury awards $5 million in non-covered damages does not mean you will ever get a dime if the insurance company will not stand behind it due to coverage defenses. It is far better to be awarded an amount to cover the costs of repair.

## Declaratory Relief

Simply put, declaratory relief is when a judge determines the parties' rights or legal obligations. When determining the insurance issues in a construction defect claim, declaratory relief can be requested to provide clarity on an insurance company's responsibility to defend an insured party against a lawsuit, pay damages, or both, before a case is settled or tried. Courts may also require the insurance company to hire a lawyer to represent the insured who has no ties with the insurance company.

## Insurance Company Duties

An insurance company must reasonably defend an insured's claim when determining its responsibility to pay damages. A part of meeting this standard is to investigate the claim filed by the insured. Since there is an obvious conflict between the insured's interests and the insurance company's interests, the insurance company has an "implied covenant of good faith and fair dealing". Insurance companies who fail to live up to their duties and good faith requirements, implied or otherwise, can be subjected to a "bad faith" lawsuit by the builder or contractors involved in any construction defect lawsuit.

Insurance bad faith matters become very complicated in themselves. Who can sue for what varies from state to state and virtually from day to day. Competent legal counsel must carefully evaluate these cases. Insurance bad faith comes into play when the developer is still in business and his insurance company will not pony up the damage money. Sometimes you can settle with the developer and as part of the settlement he will assign to you any bad faith claim he may have against his insurance company.

## Duty of Insured

Insured parties such as developers, architects, contractors, construction managers, or sub-contractors, have duties to their insurance company. First, an insured must give notice of the claim to the insurance company within a short time after the claim against the insured if filed. Second, the insured must also cooperate in the defense of a claim, including not acting in a way that would injure or impair the right of the insurance company to present the best defense. Lastly, the insured cannot enter into a settlement agreement without the participation of the insurance company and then attempt to collect what the insured pays in the settlement from the insurance company.

## Owner and Owner Association Insurance Policies and Coverage

Rarely, if ever, will the owner's or owner association's insurance policy cover damages for defective design, faulty construction, or soil settlement. Too many associations and owners are not aware of this important exclusion and go ahead and file a claim with the insurance company or broker only to be denied coverage. But, the mere filing of a claim relating to mold, faulty design, materials, or workmanship, or claims for land movement, subsidence, or soil settlement will place the carrier on notice that you are having issues with your building relating to original construction. Consult your attorney before filing a claim with an insurance carrier. Filing a claim can result in increased premiums or non-renewal of a policy, placing a high-risk category on the property, even if the insurance company pays nothing on the claim.

An association policy will cover certain items, such as sudden, unexpected, and unanticipated pipe bursts causing flooding and property damage, as well as, fire damage. But, there are so many exclusions in these policies that professional help is an important step to take before filing the actual claim. These policies have changed so much over the years that what was covered 5 years ago, is now excluded, for example, mold. Be careful of doing something that puts a policy at risk of being cancelled.

### Important Developer Policy Exclusions

Work product exclusions are found in every policy, including coverage for damages caused by the work undertaken by the insured. Over the years, insurance companies have become creative with policy exclusions. Many times, a developer assumes an insurance polity will provide protection, however, when a construction defect claim arises, developers are caught off guard by the policy exclusions. A broad form policy with completed operations coverage will provide greater protection. It costs more money to obtain this type of better insurance, so not every policy has completed operations coverage.

The bottom line is that the insurance industry constantly re-writes policies to restrict coverage wherever and whenever they can get away with it. Policy exclusions can include soil settlement, stacking consecutive policy limits, or, if you can believe it, for building residential projects even when the specific task was to build a residential project. Insurance companies are focused on the bottom line, and the less money they pay out, the more they keep.

## Chapter Ten Do's and Don'ts

### Do:

- Do have your attorney explain the types and nature of insurance policies involved.
- Do have your attorney explain whether and what insurance coverage is available and whether it is sufficient.
- Do choose a law firm with a proven knowledge and experience with handling insurance coverage matters.
- Do have your lawyer update insurance information regularly. A monthly status letter should address this.

### Don't:

- Don't try to decide what an insurance company's responsibility is. That is your lawyer's job.
- Don't hire a firm that is also acting as the association's counsel. They generally have limited insurance or defect litigation experience, and conflicts of interest may exist. And these firms work by the hour for the most part.

# CHAPTER ELEVEN: THE CASE IS FILED. NOW WHAT?

For any construction defect claim process, your goal is to recover what is necessary to repair the damage caused by the defects. At this point, you have gone through the steps of finding the right attorney, hiring consultants and experts, investigating the types of defects and resulting damage, determining insurance coverage and your ability to recover, going through the pre-litigation procedures, and attempting an early settlement. A generous amount of work and effort have been spent to get to this point and you are about to file your lawsuit. Now what?

## Discovery Management: Case Management Orders & Pretrial Orders

Discovery is a legal tool used by parties in a lawsuit to uncover information relevant to the claim. Experienced attorneys are adept at designing a Case Management or Pretrial Order (CMO/PTO) to include a discovery plan focused on finding what the opposition has in their possession. Simply asking for and obtaining information alone is insufficient. While we may now know the general nature of the developer's insurance, this is the opportunity to get it in writing, under oath, including producing copies of the actual policies. And, due to the technical nature of the development process, to procure copies of development and architectural plans, building specifications, government reports, Department of Real Estate filings, cost estimates, repair efforts, and so forth. An assembled team of experts and consultants will need to analyze all of this on your behalf. This, of course, takes time and money. Skilled counsel understands that discovery ought to be properly administered to control costs, encourage settlement through mediation, and ensure successful resolution.

Your defect lawyer should ask the court to appoint a special master or discovery referee early on in your claims process. Usually, there are persons available who are familiar with this area of law and have the time available handle discovery disputes and help organize the case. The benefit of a discovery referee is to help assure that discovery decisions remain fair throughout the construction defect claim process.

Check with your attorney to see if a CMO/PTO is in place. The CMO/PTO may already have named a discovery referee. However, CMO/PTO's have a broader impact because these are court orders approved by a judge. These orders are intended to guide the court and parties through the construction defect claim labyrinth with set dates and timetables the parties are required to follow, including a trial date. Without these set dates, a sense of urgency does not exist by opposing parties to provide any discovery. The end result is a claim that goes nowhere.

While you will not necessarily be involved in the day-to-day aspects of discovery, your help is needed. Discovery involves requesting and producing documents, inspection and testing protocols, taking depositions, sending out subpoenas and interrogatories, and responding to the ones your attorney will receive from the defendants in your case. Therefore, you should have a basic understanding of the discovery process and the events that could occur.

## Depositions: Tell Us What We Want to Know

A deposition is when witness testimony is taken outside of the court. Even though depositions occur in informal surroundings, the parties involved are to act as though they were conducted in court. The witness, also called a deponent, is placed under oath, can be questioned by one or more attorneys, and may be requested to provide documents. What the deponent says is taken down by a court reporter, and sometimes videotaped.

Any party to the action can depose any other person, corporate officer, or government organization that may have information. For example, your attorney may want to depose the developer's insurance broker to make sure the correct policy was provided to cover your construction defects. Deposing a party only requires a notice to the party's attorney. Before a non-party can be deposed, that person must be subpoenaed.

If your construction defect claim process has come this far, you may be involved in a deposition. Preparation is important, not only to understand what may occur in your deposition, but also to also ease any tension you may have about this procedure. Broad questions are allowed during a deposition as long as they are related to the subject matter of the lawsuit. Parties are still looking for information, thus, courts provide latitude to allow questions that can lead to the discovery of relevant information. However, if you make it to trial, only relevant questions are allowed, a rule judges strictly follow.

In addition to requiring your presence, you may be obligated to bring records, files, or other evidence to the deposition. It is very important for you to discuss this with your lawyer to be sure you bring the correct documentation. Plan on meeting with your attorney, who will explain the nature and purpose of the deposition.

## Interrogatories

Interrogatories are written questions drafted by one party with the purpose of discovering information from another party. Your attorney will want to incorporate the interrogatories into the CMO/PTO to force an answer by a certain date. Questions asked are on a wide variety of matters: times, dates, names of parties, available insurance, how the opposition plans to direct its case ("contentious interrogatories"), or to obtain information that would otherwise take time and money to research. They also are considerably less expensive than depositions because they do not require court reporters, video operators, travel expenses, or coffee and donuts for everyone.

There are disadvantages to interrogatories. Opposing parties can provide vague or evasive responses because the person who should respond will generally answer these with their attorney's assistance. Follow up questions cannot be asked to combat vague answers, nor can one deduce much about the demeanor or credibility of the witness. Spontaneity is lost without personal interaction, and rarely will the interrogatories lead to great revelations.

## Disclose Your Experts

Opposing parties will want to know who your experts are, just as you will want to know theirs. The law's disclosure requirement allows each side to depose the other's experts to discover their opinions and conclusions about your case. Some courts have very specific rules about when experts must be disclosed or lists of experts exchanged. Here as well, your attorney will want to include this request into a CMO/PTO.

## Defects, Truth, and Videotape

In certain circumstances, attorneys videotape depositions. Video also is used extensively during property inspections, to record the nature and extent of damages for study during trial preparation, and to demonstrate to the trial jury what the damages are. Rules surrounding videotape should be included in the CMO/PTO.

## Let Me See What You Have

The bottom line of the discovery process is for each side to show each other what they have. We have provided you with common discovery methods, and have explained how a CMO/PTO can provide guidance to fairly and efficiently keep the discovery process moving forward. The following are examples of other forms of discovery you will encounter during your construction defect claim process.

Under your lawyer's guidance, you, the owner association, and your property manager will assemble a great number of documents for the other side to view and copy in some manner. Anything not covered by the attorney-client privilege is game as long as it can lead to information relevant to your claim. Even emails, texts, twitters, videos, computer disks, or face book comments can be requested. A lot of work and patience will be needed on your part to help pull documents together. Counsel's staff can be a big help in this process.

Your attorney will make a document request of the developer, whose counsel is required to produce on their behalf. Let it be known that these documents can result in file cabinets full of information. Your attorney will want all drawings, plans, owner contracts, contractor and sub-contractor agreements, Department of Real Estate records, marketing brochures, memos, phone records, computer disks, photographs, video recordings, emails, and any other type of documentation or record related in any way to the developer's design and construction of your project. Your attorney, their staff, and your experts will wade through this information to reconstruct what happened in your case.

Besides documentation, you also may be requested to "produce" land or other property for inspection. Since you are the one claiming a defect, it is only reasonable that you allow the opposing party to inspect the questioned property. Inspections generally take two steps. First, sight inspections take place. The experts walk around the property, and take notes, photos, or even videos. This is followed by the next step, intrusive testing. Based on the sight inspections, as well as other forms of discovery, the experts take physical samples of the building. Again, notes, photographs, and video are used to document this step. The CMO/PTO guides the parties in this important endeavor.

## Chapter Eleven Do's and Don'ts

### Do:

- Do enter into a Case Management or Pretrial Order early in the process. .
- Do promptly provide whatever information your attorney requests.
- Do meet with your attorney before you are deposed so he or she can explain the nature and purpose and properly prepare you for the deposition.
- Do work with your lawyer to provide all documents you were requested to produce for your deposition before the deposition so he or she can decide what is relevant and what should or should not be provided to the opposition.
- Do cooperate to provide access for on site inspections or testing.

### Don't:

- Don't act slowly regarding discovery requests. There are time limits involved and missing them can harm your case.
- Don't withhold information from your attorney because you believe it is harmful to your case. That will cause more harm than good.

# CHAPTER TWELVE:
# STATUTE OF LIMITATIONS

A statute of limitations is a specific time period to bring a claim. Generally, for construction defect claims, legislative acts state the specific time periods one has to bring a lawsuit. The rationale behind time limits is that people, corporations, and other legal entities should not be forever liable for their acts and omissions. Over time, witnesses die or leave the area, memories fade, and documents get lost, all of which can make it difficult, if not impossible, to defend a lawsuit. In addition, it is thought that there should come a time when potential defendants should no longer be under the threat of the continuing possibility of a lawsuit. While courts enforce statutes of limitations, generally they abhor denying plaintiffs their day in court because of a legal technicality. Neither do courts want plaintiffs – either because of ignorance, oversight, or simple tardiness – to be able to win lawsuits simply because vital evidence has disappeared.

Not surprisingly, the construction, development, and insurance industries seem to perpetually lobby legislative bodies to shorten these time limits. They argue that plaintiffs who know of a problem should not be allowed to sit on their rights for such a long period of time that it could place potential defendants at a serious disadvantage.

Consumer groups counter industry arguments by illustrating the difficulties to protect oneself with a shortened statute of limitations. Consumers may not even be aware of a defect – let alone of their right of a remedy – before the statute of limitations expires. Construction, development, and insurance industries understand the difficult nature inherent with discovering when a construction defect is known. They are also fully aware that shortening the statute of limitations helps their overall goal to limit their liability for their defective products by making it as difficult as possible to bring a lawsuit.

Compounding an already difficult legal issue is the different statute of limitations jurisdictions have for the same claim and the fact that different actions in the same lawsuit have different statutes of limitations. These time limits are constantly changing, which means that you need a smart lawyer who stays abreast of the latest developments.

Just as a statute of limitation ends, it also has to begin, and determining when it begins, can be equally as confusing as figuring out when it ends. In construction defect cases, the statutes generally begin upon "substantial completion" or "close of escrow" of the home or condo, phrases with very technical and precise legal meanings, determined by a series of factors.

Another factor that can be involved is the concept of "repose," which is similar to a statute of limitations, but does not require a showing of knowledge. For example, a statute of limitations may say that a buyer has one, two, four, or five years to file a claim on a specific defect, or that the suit must be filed within ten years of "substantial completion." In this example, the ten-year period is a statute of repose.

Deciding the meaning of all these terms and issues surrounding statutes of limitations requires careful, close legal analysis and should be left to an attorney with considerable expertise in the area. In California, the legislature enacted SB 800 (Civil Code Section 895) to provide direction for the construction defect claims process, including statue of limitations. Before we look at these statutes of limitations, you should note that condo-conversions and homes or condos with singed purchase agreements preceding January 1, 2003 do not fall within SB 800 and will rely on the traditional ten-year statute of limitations. For more on this, see Appendix C.

SB 800 not only listed all actionable defects, but, it assigned the defects to a one, two, four, five, and ten year statute of limitations. Generally, these time limits start with when the notice of completion or occupancy was filed with the appropriate government agency. Be aware of these time limits because some damages may not be recoverable after a short period of time. Even though the statute defines a beginning and end, there are factors you should be aware of that affect these time limits.

The first effect on the time limit we'll discuss relates to owner associations. A common practice is for a developer to have control over the owner association for some time after a project is completed. The clock does not begin on the SB 800 time limits until after the developer relinquishes control of the board. This can have a profound effect by giving owners more time in which they can bring a claim.

The next issue we'll discuss relates to discovery of a defect. While SB 800 provides time limits within which a claim must be brought, California Code of Civil Procedure Section 338 states that you must bring a claim for damage to property within three years from the date of discovery of each defect. So, if you discover, or should have discovered, for example, a ten-year defect in year two, your must file a claim on that defect by year 5. You cannot sit on your rights, expecting the court to allow you to wait until year eight or nine to file a claim you knew about years earlier. For an association board, notice of the defect can come from various sources: management, construction or design professionals, repair contractors, and even the owners in the association. Evidence of repairs, versus normal maintenance, to various components of the building can be used to prove the association board should have known of a defect, and may trigger the three-year time limit of the California Code of Civil Procedure Section 338. So, a word of caution: be very vigilant with and pay attention to repair invoices and reports that come your way suggesting that the repairs were the result of original construction deficiencies. Defense attorneys spend a lot of time reviewing association documents, minutes, and records to find such evidence. It can be fatal to your claim. Always protect reports or other evidence of possible construction defects or deficiencies by sending such reports to your attorney first in order to evaluate the information. For example, if you ask for an experienced repair contractor to evaluate a roof leak, and he reports back that the roof as originally installed was defective, have that report sent only to counsel. Counsel can advise you if this report triggers any statute of limitations and might ask to see if there are any other repair records or reports of similar deficiencies, so you are adequately protected and timely file your claim. Also, if the developer comes out to repair the problem, the time by which you must bring a claim may be extended for the length of time repairs are promised or undertaken, but only as to the defect repaired.

The three year rule can be problematic when a statute of limitations begins running unbeknownst to the association board members or other owners in a community. Be wary of developers who have been known to send people out to ask owner association members when they first noticed a defect. If the association has hundreds of members, the developer may find one or two owners claiming to have known of the problem for years, even if he or she has no idea of its cause. For this and other reasons, owners should not speak to anyone other than representatives of their lawyer's firm or owner association's board members. Written instructions should go out to all owners to alert them on how they should respond in this situation.

This discussion above is a basic overview that we hope provided some understanding of an important legal issue. One of the worst things that can happen to a plaintiff is to miss a statutory time limit.

### Chapter Twelve Do's and Don'ts

### Do:

- Do seek independent legal advice as soon as you suspect a construction defect to avoid losing your rights. Some statutes of limitations can begin within one or two years from the date of completion or close of escrow by the first buyer.
- Do know that if an expert, contractor, or home inspector looked at your home and provided a report, your statute may be running. You can protect the privacy of this information by having the expert and his or her report sent to your lawyer when it is complete.

### Don't:

- Don't try to figure out for yourself whether the statute of limitations or period of response has run. Leave that to your attorney.
- Don't turn over an expert or contractor's report or repair estimate to a developer. It may trigger a statute of limitations.

# CHAPTER THIRTEEN: DAMAGES

When discussing damages in a construction defect claim, you are talking about money. The general purpose of damages is to make the injured party "whole" again, or to return the party to its position before the injury or loss. In these types of claims, this is generally the amount it takes to repair the defect. Before going any further, you must always remember, and this is an issue have we previously discussed, to never "gold plate", or artificially inflate, your damages. This tactic requires stretching the truth and lying, it will backfire, and you may end up loosing your ability to recover anything.

## Damages As Prescribed By Law

California construction defect claims allow damages as defined in SB 800 (Civil Code Section 895) for homes and condos completed or closed escrow after January 1, 2003. The language used can be found in section 944:

> "If a claim for damages is made under this title, the homeowner is only entitled to damages for the reasonable value of repairing any violation of the standards set forth in this title, the reasonable cost of repairing any damages caused by the repair efforts, the reasonable cost of repairing and rectifying any damages resulting from the failure of the home to meet the standards, the reasonable cost of removing and replacing any improper repair by the builder, reasonable relocation and storage expenses, lost business income if the home was used as a principal place of a business licensed to be operated from the home, reasonable investigative costs for each established violation, and all other costs or fees recoverable by contract or statute."

## Cost of Repairs Versus Diminution of Value

Plaintiffs in construction defect complaints usually request "cost of repairs" damages. A cost of repair damage calculation is based on what it takes to repair your home, condo, or common area. 95 percent of construction defect claims use this calculation. Your cost of repair estimate will come from your experts, who in turn use their investigation findings to determine what is wrong and what it will take to fix it.

Diminution of value claims are used when a home or condo is beyond repair, or the value is reduced. Even though this is seldom used, it can be a significant damage. If a repair is not possible, because your home is built near an earthquake fault or toxic dump site, and the existence of the fault or dump causes a reduction in your home's value, then you would claim diminished value. If the value of your house new was $500,000, and later you discover the nearby earthquake fault, which the developer either knew about or should have known about, the value of your home could be reduced by half. This loss of $250,000 has to be made up to you from somewhere. Here as well, your experts will provide the necessary evidence based on their investigations to back up your claim.

Both cost of repair and diminution of value damages claims are allowed in California's SB 800 (Civil Code Section 895). For more on this, see Appendix C.

## Stigma – Or, If It Happened Before, It Could Happen Again

Suppose repairs are made, but your home still is reduced in value because a potential buyer is fearful that the injury, such as a landslide or earthquake, could occur? This is referred to as a "stigma" on the property. Some courts will allow recovery for it. Recent case law, however, has limited stigma damages to more catastrophic problems.

## Attorney Fees

Attorney fees are generally not recoverable in California. However, it is always a good idea to carefully read your association's CC&R's to determine if there are any rights to fees established.

## Expert Fees and Costs

The prevailing party in a construction defect case frequently will recover expert fees and related costs. Because of the size and complexity of construction defect cases, these fees and costs can be considerable. In Section 944 of SB 800, the California Legislature allows your expert fees and costs to be recovered as damages. These are commonly referred to as "Stearman Costs".

## Punitive Damages

Courts do not like to allow punitive damages. In California, plaintiffs must show by clear and convincing evidence that the defendant was guilty of fraud, malice, or oppression. Other states have different standards for punitive damages.

In California, an advantage of receiving punitive damages, besides the extra compensation, is that sometimes the plaintiff will be able to be compensated for attorney's fees. However, insurance companies generally will not cover, and, thus, not pay punitive damages.

## Chapter Thirteen Do's and Don'ts

### Do:

- Do help your attorney prepare as quickly and effectively as possible.
- 
- Do have your attorney explain all potential settlement possibilities and methods.

### Don't:

- Don't attempt to calculate the value of your damages. That is a job for your attorney and experts.
- 
- Don't hesitate to tell your expert or your attorney of any potential damages.

# CHAPTER FOURTEEN: WHO WANTS TO GO TO COURT?

Over 95 percent of construction defect cases never go to trial. Almost always, parties to a defect case would rather mediate and settle the case rather than run the risk of going to trial. For plaintiffs, there is the chance a verdict or judgment will be well below what is needed for repair, and for defendants the possibility of an unexpectedly large award looms. In short, jury decisions are extremely hard to predict. As a result, owners and owner associations should have a familiarity with how cases are resolved outside of a courtroom.

## Settlement Strategies

Early preparation is the single most important factor in getting a case to early settlement. This means your lawyer should understand the various tasks that occur in a short period of time: gather experts, begin statutory pretrial steps, conduct discovery under a Case Management or Pretrial Order (CMO/PTO), review damage claim reports and repair estimates, understand available insurance, and create settlement strategies. Only then can one make the subtlest of responsible settlement overtures.

An experienced attorney will understand how to control the pace of your claim, but defense counsel will frequently act in ways to slow the process. Defendants believe the more they can prolong a case, the more eager the plaintiffs will be to settle for a lower amount. An example of how defense attorneys attempt to slow down the process is by bringing in new defendants, such as subcontractors, engineers, manufacturers, and project managers. Without setting any benchmarks, like those found in a CMO/PTO, parties do not have to act, and the claim will continue longer than necessary.

A skilled plaintiff's attorney can circumvent defense counsel's effort to slow the process, or at least lessen the impact, by creating a sense of urgency on all parties, named or not, with a CMO/PTO. The CMO/PTO is a court order that sets up all of the important dates for a construction defect claim, including a trial date. In California, if a case is deemed complex, a CMO/PTO is automatic. When a claim is not deemed complex, your attorney has to ask for the CMO/PTO to be put in place. Because most construction defect claims involve multiple parties, judges want an organized process, and typically find it in the court's best interest to encourage these orders. The result of a CMO/PTO can be to reach a settlement on your claim within 18-24 months. Without this order and set dates, your chances of an early settlement diminish rapidly.

If the defense is quickly forced to trial, they will be fearful of a large jury award. Look at it as a football game: The offense wants to get a touchdown as quickly as possible, the defense wants to eat up as much time as possible to prevent the touchdown. It is only when you are in a scoring position that the opposition will be ready to discuss settlement.

Your attorney's job is to organize the offense and to educate the opposition to the strengths of your claims. If you and your lawyer present a persuasive argument and it becomes apparent you have a winning case, the question is not if the case will settle, but what the settlement will be. You must, therefore, work as closely as possible with your attorney to prepare the case as quickly as possible.

## Jointly Retained Experts

Often, once settlement begins, the primary dispute is either the amount of settlement or the type and scope of anticipated repairs. The result can be an impasse with neither side willing to budge, particularly if the sides are too far apart.

The parties can overcome the standoff by having the court or mediator appoint a joint expert to review the paperwork, plans, specifications, reports, testing results, and any other relevant documentation involved. Both plaintiffs and defendants participate in the selection process with the help of a mediator or judge.

It is important to both sides of the action that they choose experts who have neither strong plaintiff nor defense bias. If the expert's opinion on repairs and necessary costs obviously favors one party, it is doubtful the expert will be acceptable to all parties.

Usually, using jointly retained experts happens only in the early stages of litigation and requires that all the parties trust each other to live up to their agreement. This agreement, of course, should be in writing.

## Large Developers Who Want to Keep Their Reputations

Large, active, and reputable developers find it in their self-interest to maintain consumer goodwill and preserve their own good name. These desires enter into settlement negotiations in two ways. First, in projects that are sold in phases, the California State Department of Real Estate can review a developer's representations in completed housing phases to see if there could be a pattern of misrepresentation stretching to uncompleted phases. In addition, when a developer submits a subdivision approval application, the developer must guarantee that no known defects exist when the homes are sold. If a defect exists and misrepresentations are alleged, the Department of Real Estate can investigate, and decide to stop construction and sale of future stages. Then, the developer may have to make significant changes in the design or construction technique. A developer would loose considerable time and money were this to happen.

The second way reputation enters in settlement is the strain on resources a lawsuit can cause. If it is apparent, especially early in litigation, that there is a defect and most likely the developer eventually will lose in court, settlement will save a lot of trouble. In these types of settlements, the developers usually require individual owners or owner associations keep the settlement terms confidential. This allows the developers both to settle and keep their good reputation intact.

## Owner Association Settlements

Depending on how property is held, the board of an owner association frequently has the power to settle the claim. In this case, owners and the association's board of directors must work closely together to assure a just settlement.

Less frequently, these two parties have conflicts of interest. In those cases, each entity will have separate attorneys to help eliminate further conflicts. In most common interest developments this is rare because the owner association brings the action for common area defects and the owner owns only the air space inside the unit.

## Cash or Carry For Single Family Homes?

Monetary settlements are not the only settlement possibility. Fairly sophisticated methods of settling a dispute can be employed. The developer can offer the individual owner the replacement property of equivalent value and guarantee the same monthly payment, a certain number of payments, and interest. There are disadvantages to this settlement method. For example, it may require a move to a different neighborhood and a change of schools, and new friends for you and your children. Even a move nearby can be a stressful and expensive process.

Another settlement alternative is for the developer to agree to pay money over time, usually by purchasing an annuity. This is especially useful if defects are anticipated in the future because of design or construction problems.

Settling claims of individual defects separately sometimes is a useful strategy. Some claims, such as leaky roofs, require quick repair. Others, such as land subsidence or structural problems, can be settled at a later time. This allows the developer to quickly settle claims believed to be legitimate, and also helps the owners and owner associations repair particular defects quickly and efficiently. You need to be cautious about watering down your claim by settling the most serious and compelling problems, leaving the more challenging ones to prove.

## Getting It All Down

Settlement terms are always reduced to writing, and a request to dismiss any lawsuit is filed with the court. The settlement terms are then incorporated into a release that is signed by all of the parties agreeing to the settlement.

One type of release, called a general release, should be entered into with caution. A general release frees defendants from all liability for any past, present, and future liability. There could be undiscovered defects for which the developer will be escaping liability. You should be sure your attorney explains to you all the terms of any release you consider signing. Among the questions you should ask your lawyer are:

- Who does the release cover?
- What defects does the release cover?
- When does the release go into effect?
- How does the release cover unknown damages?
- If the release does cover undiscovered or future defects (a general release), why should I sign it?

Even though a general release can be tricky, singing one may be a reasonable step to settle your claim. After thorough and careful investigations by your experts, assuring you have no other defects or that defects should not be expected may provide the necessary comfort to sign a general release.

## The Enforcer

Get an agreement on the record in front of the judge and in open court where all parties appear and agree to the terms. Then, get a written settlement agreement that contains provisions to enforce the settlement terms and to allow the court in which the case is brought to retain jurisdiction, and therefore the authority, to enforce the settlement. The parties will want to place any agreement into the trial court record in case of future problems. Generally, settlements are enforced as contracts, but if it is a court order, the party or party's attorney violating the settlement could be held in contempt of court and have sanctions imposed.

## Owner Association Rules

California law requires the owner association, under Civil Code Section 1375.1, to follow special disclosure procedures when settling a lawsuit. At the very least, the board of directors should approve the agreement and advise all owners of the terms.

## Alternative Dispute Resolution

Recent years have seen clogged court calendars, a rise in expensive and time-consuming pretrial discovery, and an increase in pretrial motions and legal maneuvering. This can cause the expenses to balloon, and it can take longer to get a case to trial. It also means more and more cases are decided on narrow legal issues often full of procedural problems.

When the consumer actually gets his or her day in court, the issues can be too complex for most juries and judges to understand. Judges, who seldom have a construction defect litigation background, must be brought up to speed. Juries, usually consisting of average citizens, often have an even bigger challenge trying to understand these cases.

Many litigants, unhappy with the current legal system, have turned to Alternate Dispute Resolution (ADR), which can quickly, fairly, and economically resolve the cases outside of court. ADR also allows the parties to solve their disputes amicably. Developers, after all, are in business to build homes, not to be involved in litigation, and owners and board members want to live their lives without the stress of lawsuits hanging over their heads.

An astute attorney understands the stresses on a court's time, and will include an ADR into a Case Management Order or Pretrial Order (CMO/PTO). ADR provides many types of formats as alternatives to trial. Mediation and special settlement conferences with the use of retired judges or impartial disinterested attorneys are among the more popular methods for dispute resolution. Usually there are costs involved, including fees paid to lawyers, retired judges, other professionals, and mediation services. Customarily, these costs are split among the parties. A CMO/PTO will outline the costs and how much each party is to pay.

Another benefit of ADR is that court evidence rules can be arbitrary and prevent some information from reaching the jury. ADR is much more informal and allows the parties to argue their cases with fewer restrictions. Your attorney should include ADR procedures in the CMO/PTO. Again, having all of these issues spelled out up front leads to a quicker resolution of your claim.

## Mediation

Mediation is an extremely useful tool, and a non-binding process where the mediator attempts to bring the parties to agreement. The parties retain the right to accept or reject the settlement offers. All discussions are confidential and cannot be used at trial. Mediators vary in their persuasive abilities, and some parties are more eager to settle than others. It generally occurs in a casual environment with both lawyers and parties present. Mediation resolves 95% of all disputes. Use it often and freely. Mediation is the preferred method because it will lead to a more timely resolution of your claim

## Arbitration

Sometimes after a defect is discovered or, often, when a home is purchased, the homebuyer is forced to binding arbitration for any disputes. Arbitration has rules similar to court rules, but generally they are slightly less rigid and more open to interpretation. Recent court rulings have found forced arbitration provisions unfair, invalid, and unenforceable against owners and owner associations.

## Voluntary Settlement Conferences

Even though mandatory settlement conferences are required before trial, many courts allow, and even encourage, voluntary settlement conferences. These are very similar to and sometimes combined with mediation. The parties agree on the rules, retain a retired jurist or other trusted person to preside, and proceed. Usually, the settlement judge listens to each side and then gives his opinion of how a judge and jury would rule. Sometimes, mediators will team up with the trial courts judge to help settle the case. The overriding goal is to bring the parties together and resolve their differences.

## General Reference

The parties may agree to enter into a procedure called "general reference," which is an agreement to decide certain issues—lawyers learn in law school how to spot issues—by asking the court to appoint a referee to rule on particular questions. These rulings and findings by the referee are unchangeable at trial.

In general reference, the parties also can reserve certain issues to be ruled on in court. This can save considerable time and money by shortening the time attorneys and experts spend in trial.

## Chapter Fourteen Do's and Don'ts

### Do:

- Do consider alternate settlement strategies and discuss them with your lawyer early on in your case. 95% of cases settle before trial.
- Do remember that defendants have just as much to lose from a jury verdict as you do, even though juries tend to favor owners over developers when mistakes are made.
- Do realize that defendants may be as eager to enter into alternate settlement strategies as you are. Mediation is the preferred method.
- Do discuss any release of liability with your attorney very carefully.

### Don't:

- Don't be surprised if your case never makes it to trial. Over 95% of all cases settle.
- Don't forget to provide as much help as you can to your attorney. Early preparation encourages early and successful settlement.
- Don't enter into settlement negotiations without your attorney.

# CHAPTER FIFTEEN: CONCLUSION - OR, THE STORY CONTINUES

Congratulations for making it this far. We hope you have a better understanding of some of the ins and outs surrounding a construction defects claims process. If you want a truer taste of a defect case take a look at the construction defect textbook we wrote for other lawyers and judges, *Handling Construction Defect Claims: Western States* (Wiley Publications, 1999, 3rd ed., Supplemented Annually).

Fortunately, lawyers and courts are compelled to act according to the facts of each case. When those facts are applied to law is the point where elasticity of the laws can be seen to raise the suitably simple to the height of the incredibly complex. Using Ockham Razor's logic premise that says the simplest answer is always the best answer, may apply in philosophy, but seems to be useless in litigation. Why?

Partly, it is because lawyers enjoy seeing both subtlety and complexity. Partly, it is because of the linguistic development of the words lawyers use, who, as paraphrased by Strunk and White's Elements of Style, tend to be drawn to five-dollar Latin-based verbiage to express half-dollar ideas because historically the educated in our culture spoke in Latin or Greek, even though the people spoke in English. Mostly however, it is because the legal principles must be applied to a virtually infinite number of fact situations and constantly changing societal and social needs.

Almost always, lawyers learn intellectual purity in law school, only to discover after graduation that few cases even resemble the ones they studied. Practicing law is like playing a baseball game where the batter is seldom presented with a simple fastball. Instead, lawyers are almost always thrown curves, sliders, change-ups, knuckleballs, and the occasional screwball for confusion.

We see this by examining the development of construction defect law. Originally, the homebuyers would go to a craftsman builder, tell him what they wanted, then wait and watch while the house was built. These charming houses, discernible by their attention to detail, hardwood floors, and plaster interior walls, can be found in every city in America.

If one of these houses was poorly built, the consumer sued the builder under the law of contracts. He would tell the court that he agreed to give the builder money in exchange for the builder constructing a home. The buyer would say that they had a contract and the builder breached that contract. The buyer, however, was stuck with the theory of *caveat emptor*.

What happened if the house was built, but not built as well as should be? The buyer could claim that the builder was negligent: the contractor had a duty to build a decent house, and in some important way he breached that duty causing damage. For example, the builder may have had a duty to use decent cured lumber but instead, to save a few dollars, used green lumber, which cracked under the building's weight. Pretty simple. Right? Ah, but now come the curve balls. What if the person stuck with the faulty housing is not the original buyer? What if a builder can't be shown to be negligent in a particular way, but the house is defective anyway.

After WWII, housing began to be mass-produced, just like most things in a world of convenience. Custom-built homes became a privilege of the rich or, occasionally the merely eccentric. The mass-produced home even got a name, tract housing, and made for instant neighborhoods. Next came planned unit developments, which owned the communal roadways, swimming pools, spas, and other amenities. And when cities filled up, luxury high-rise buildings, once the domain of business, became a new type of mass-produced condominium, and old buildings no longer in use as factories were converted into a new use, housing. The shifts in housing types presented new and challenging issues for consumers, lawyers, and courts.

New building techniques also created problems. Understanding these new construction methods required lawyers and courts to expand their areas of expertise. Housing was being built on hillsides and in valleys that were either carved out of land previously too steep to be built upon, or on fill materials used to level canyons and dried riverbeds. Suddenly, geotechnical and civil engineers became required for many claims and created additional litigation expenses.

Also, builders started using space-age building methods and materials, which caused environmental and other problems. New roofing materials and other coverings created water-intrusion problems that resulted in mold, mildew, and rot. These problems meant the law had to be redesigned and restructured as well. Legal principles were expanded from contract law all the way to strict liability.

Construction defect law is still expanding and evolving. Under pressure from insurance companies over he last decade, the legislatures in many states have spent considerable time and effort re-evaluating the entire American tort system. It seems during every election, our courts are under fire from all directions by well-funded building industry groups who either want to significantly limit or even eliminate consumers' rights to redress. In California, the laws are well settled for the time being with the advent of SB 800 (Civil Code Section 895) along with the abundance of case law to define owners' rights.

Of course, limiting Americans' rights to gain access to our legal system would be disastrous to consumer rights. Homebuyers will be prey to unethical developers who seek to increase profits to the detriment of consumers. For more on this, see Appendix E.

Such limitations eventually would effect other consumer protections. People injured by dangerous products or poisonous medications, or have consumed tainted foods, might lose access to legal redress. Also, victims of other types of accidents may be forced to endure lifetime problems, and many other injured consumers may be prevented from receiving compensation.

Luckily, our judicial system has stood firm against these onslaughts, primarily because the American voter has a deep and abiding belief in fair play and aspires to partake in the American Dream of home ownership. Because of this belief, when new homebuyers invest their life savings in new homes, they can get what they pay for and have rights to redress for any problems that might arise.

# APPENDIX

# APPENDIX A: ATTORNEY SELECTION CRITERIA & ONLINE RESOURCES

| ATTORNEY SELECTION CRITERIA | THE MILLER LAW FIRM | OTHERS |
|---|---|---|
| Preeminent AV Rated, the highest possible peer rating for legal ability and ethical practice by Martindale-Hubbel. | YES | |
| Peer review rated California Super Lawyer (2007-2010). | YES | |
| Pioneered construction defect litigation in the early 1980's after working as a developer's attorney in the 1970's. Understands both sides of the claim process. | YES | |
| Author of the definitive Legal Treatise on construction defect litigation, the book used by judges, mediators, and lawyers. | YES | |
| Maintains a Multi-Million line of credit to withstand even the most aggressive defense tactics. | YES | |
| Works on a 100% contingency fee, deferring all attorneys' fees to the end. No hourly fees are charged. | YES | |
| Advances all litigation and expert costs. | YES | |
| Well known and respected by developers, their insurance companies, and their defense attorneys for the past 30 years. | YES | |
| Obtains largest per unit recovery of all defect counsel. | YES | |
| Practices only in California, keeping resources and lawyers focused on local and regional issues. | YES | |
| Conducts extensive due diligence to understand issues and determine likelihood of success. | YES | |

| | | |
|---|---|---|
| Transparency with client: monthly board letters, monthly accounting, quarterly disclosures to homeowners, owner meetings at the case beginning and conclusion, HOA expert consulting budget. | YES | |
| Hires and manages time of the most qualified and well-respected experts to conduct the defect investigation. | YES | |
| Assists client before and during mediation to take guesswork out of determining the correct, responsible settlement value. | YES | |
| Over 97% of cases settle within 18-24 months. | YES | |
| Assists client with selecting reconstruction company for repairs after settlement is reached. | YES | |
| A significant track record of recovery in defect litigation of over $500 Million. | YES | |

## ONLINE RESOURCES

To better help you understand your rights, obligations, and legal options when selecting a law firm, consider the following resources:

1. Consumer Attorneys of California (CAOC)

   www.caoc.com/CA/

   www.caoc.com/CA/index.cfm?event=showPage&pg=selectlawyer

   www.caoc.com/CA/index.cfm?event=showPage&pg=contingencyFees

   www.caoc.com/CA/index.cfm?event=showPage&pg=feekey

2. The State Bar of California

   www.calbar.ca.gov/

   • http://ethics.calbar.ca.gov/

   • http://rules.calbar.ca.gov/LinkClick.aspx?fileticket=8qtNkWP-Kjw%3d&tabid=1233

3. Is Your Association Lawyer Splitting Fees, What to Ask and What to Know, by James I. Ham & Ellen A. Pansky, Esq.

   www.constructiondefects.com/documents/Doc2.pdf

# APPENDIX B: TWELVE MOST ASKED QUESTIONS AND ANSWERS

The following questions offer broad information for various topics in construction defects. Most of what is discussed here is developed further in various parts of this book.

## 1. What is a construction defect?

Almost any condition that reduces the value of a home, condominium, or common area can be legally recognized as a *defect in design or workmanship*, or a *defect related to land movement.* Prior to 2003, Courts recognized these two primary categories of defects for which damages are recoverable by the owner or owner association.

*Defects in design, workmanship and materials:* These include, water seepage through roofs, windows, and sliding glass doors; siding and stucco deficiencies; slab leaks or cracks; faulty drainage; improper landscaping and irrigation; termite infestation; improper materials; structural failure or collapse; defective mechanical and plumbing; faulty electrical wiring; inadequate environmental controls; improper security measures and devices; insufficient insulation and poor sound protection; and inadequate firewall protection.

*Landslide and earth settlement problems:* Examples are expansive soils; underground water or streams; landslides; settlement; earth movement; improper compaction; inadequate grading; and drainage.

Structural failures and earth movement conditions can be catastrophic in nature and present both personal injury and substantial property damage exposure. Landslide and settlement conditions may result in collapse of buildings; cracks in slabs, walls, foundations, and ceilings; disturbance of public or private utilities; and sometimes a complete undermining of the structures.

## HOME AND CONDO DEFECTS

In California, for any home or condo purchased after January 1, 2003, SB 800 (Civil Code Section 895) clarified the types of defects that the builders are responsible to fix. This statute in Sections 896 and 897 takes the guesswork out of defining a defect and clearly identifies all categories of defects for which the developer is responsible.

### 2. What does the builder's warranty really cover?

Try to read the warranty. Every warranty is different in what is covered and what is not, how long the warranty lasts, and what the builder will do to fix construction problems. Most will not address ninety percent of typical construction defects. Many require you to arbitrate and give up your right to sue in court. Read the fine print because it may state that you also may end up paying the developer's arbitration costs if you lose. Do not be duped into believing they will repair defects to your satisfaction. The warranty is more a marketing tool than any real effort to address serious problems in your home. Most developers' concept of what constitutes a construction defect falls far short of what most building standards and state statutes, like the California SB 800 (Civil Code Section 895), consider to be construction defect.

### 3. How do I prove that a defect exists?

In most cases, you will need to hire the services of an independent expert. Experts are those who have the necessary training, education, and experience to give testimony in court as to the cause of a defect. For example, if your roof leaks, a waterproofing expert who has designed effective roofs, evaluated other defective roof systems, and knows how roofs should be built would be in a good position to testify. And while a general or roofing contractor can repair a damaged roof, he may not be the best person to act as your expert. Your lawyer cannot, in most cases, prove his case against the developer unless he has a qualified expert. Experts are available in nearly every aspect of residential construction. An expert's services usually run from $150.00 to $300.00 or more per hour. California SB 800 (Civil Code Section 895) allows for these fees to be recovered in a construction defect claim. Caution: consult with counsel before hiring an expert to protect the information and control the expenses.

## 4. What kinds of damages can I recover in a lawsuit, and can I recover attorney's fees?

All courts are clear in awarding owners and owner associations the cost of repairing the defects. You can also recover whatever reasonable fees you have had to pay for your experts to investigate the cause of your defects and their costs in supervising the repairs. The costs of doing temporary repairs during and before the lawsuit to prevent further damage are also recoverable. If repairs require owners to vacate their homes, these relocation costs are included. Punitive damages, or damages awarded to punish the developer and to deter similar conduct in the future, may be awarded where the developer defendant has defrauded the buyer. With few exceptions, attorney's fees are generally not recoverable but are negotiated in every settlement by experienced counsel. In California, recoverable damages can now be found in SB 800 (Civil Code Section 895).

## 5. What should I do if the developer has agreed to make the necessary repairs?

It is wise to consult an experienced lawyer who can assist in locating an independent expert (one who has no relationship with the developer) to evaluate the developer's investigation of the problem and his proposed repair. The same expert should oversee actual repairs. Once repairs are agreed upon, the attorney can draft a proper settlement agreement that does not release the developer of liability except for the limited and defined repairs being made, and then only after the repairs have proved effective. And under SB 800 (Civil Code Section 895), repairs made by a developer pursuant to this statutory "right to repair" law does not require a release at all. The developer working outside of SB 800 (Civil Code Section 895) typically demands a broad form general release of all future liability in exchange for making repairs. Such a release may result in board of director liability and eliminate your right to sue for other defects that appear during the time remaining on your statutes of limitation. For that reason such a release is rarely, if ever, recommended. In other words, insist on a specific limited release and negotiate from there.

## 6. How long do I have to file a lawsuit?

All construction defect cases are covered by a statute of limitations. In California, for new homes sold after January 1, 2003, the rule is now found in SB 800 (Civil Code Section 895). It provides for one, two, four, five, and ten-year statutes of limitations. Before Jan 1, 2003, your statute of limitation is still generally ten years maximum from the date of completion, with some exceptions.

Under California Code of Civil Procedure Section 338, you are required to file within three years from the time you first discovered each defect. Under the three-year rule, California courts determine when "discovery" of a defect occurs. Generally, the owner must have known or observed a condition or been placed on notice of a defect. However, letters to the developer, surveys of owners' complaints, boards of directors' minutes, committee reports, reserve studies, maintenance invoices, and experts' reports may prove a defect has been discovered. Upon discovery of the defect, take prompt, appropriate action to protect your rights. By all means, before you start your claims process, get it in writing from your lawyer that none of these time limits have been blown. Don't try to analyze statute of limitations legal issues. They are very complex and require expert legal opinion.

## 7. How much will a lawsuit cost?

The total cost of prosecuting a lawsuit will depend on a number of factors, including the nature and amount of damages, the number of parties, and the attitude of the parties. Some lawsuits are settled within a relatively short period of time, while others are not resolved until just before trial. Lawsuits can be expensive, and close cooperation between owners, the owner association board of directors, the property manager, and attorney is necessary to contain the costs as much as possible. One of the major costs is hiring expert consultants; these costs are usually recoverable in the lawsuit. Experts' costs will depend upon the nature and extent of defects and the size of the project. Attorneys generally either bill by the hour or take a percentage of any recovery. If the attorney charges by the hour, expect to pay between $250 and $450 or more per hour for one with substantial experience. If the attorney works on a contingency basis, expect the fee to be 33% or more of the gross recovery. These fees are negotiable. Whatever the agreement, get it in writing. Most owners prefer the attorney to take the risk and ask for a contingency contract. Under a contingency agreement, if you don't get paid, your lawyer doesn't get paid.

## 8. Where do I get the money to pay for a lawsuit?

If your property has an owner association, several ways exist to raise money for pursuing your legal rights. First, your association's reserves are a good source. California allows associations to borrow for reserves as long as it is paid pack in a limited amount of time. Another source is to increase your monthly assessments by the percentage allowed in your CC&R's or pass a special assessment. Finally, certain lenders will finance the investigation, securing the loan with the potential recovery. You also can ask your lawyer to advance expenses. Contingency lawyers typically have a line of credit from which the expert fees and costs can be advanced to the client. If you are involved in a class action, these costs are split among all the participants. The larger the group of owners, the less you will be responsible to pay in costs.

## 9. How do I recover if the builder/developer is out of business, cannot be located, or is bankrupt?

Owner associations and owners should carefully assess the developer's ability to pay damages. The most important asset in many states is the developer's insurance. Even if the developer cannot be located or is bankrupt, the insurance companies must defend and pay claims that are covered under the policy(s). Determine early on how much insurance the developer maintained from completion of construction to the present and how much is left. It is critical to evaluate the developer's insurance, as well as, insurance for the general contractor, subcontractors, architect, engineers, and project manager. Beware of policy exclusions. Insurance companies are writing more exclusions into these policies every year.

## 10. Will an owner's or owner association's insurance companies cover damages caused by construction defects?

Not usually. The language in most owner and owner association insurance (first person) policies excludes coverage for faulty design, workmanship or materials. Disaster coverage (flood, disaster coverage, earthquake, and hurricane) must be separately evaluated.

## 11. Am I required to make repairs while the lawsuit is pending, and can I recover those costs in the lawsuit?

Yes and yes. You are required to take all reasonable steps to protect the property from sustaining additional damage. These costs are recoverable in the lawsuit. Carefully review any temporary repair program with an expert to guarantee correct documentation of the repairs.

## 12. Can I sell or refinance my home during the litigation?

The owner association board of directors has a fiduciary duty to investigate owner complaints of common area construction defects and timely pursue a claim against the developer to recover damages to fix the problems. During this time, an owner must disclose to a potential buyer common area defects and litigation. Such disclosures may have an impact on sales, but so will the condition of the home when you fill out a residential disclosure statement and hand it to a prospective buyer. Consult a real estate broker who is experienced in working with homes in litigation. Due to fluctuating interest rates, many owners may want to refinance. While in litigation, lenders are cautious about refinancing. Consult with an experienced mortgage broker. These are challenging times for borrowers and banks have tightened their lending guidelines.

# APPENDIX C: SB 800
# (CIVIL CODE SECTION 895)

For the entire statute, please visit our website at www.constructionde-fects.com. The summary below provides a quick glance of important defini-tions for every home, condo, or common area completed or closed escrow on or after January 1, 2003:

## Close of Escrow-Section 895(e)

With respect to an association, "close of escrow" means the date of sub-stantial completion or the date the builder relinquished control over the association's ability to decide whether to initiate a claim under this title, whichever is later.

## Builder Defined-Section 896

"Builder" means a builder, developer, or original seller and applies to the sale of new residential units on or after January 1, 2003. California Civil Code Sec. 911, 938. This statute does not apply to a converter or to the manufacturer of a product located within the home.

## Notice Requirements-Section 910

Prior to filing an action, the claimant shall initiate the following pre-litigation procedures:
- Written notice of the claim
- Reasonable detail of the nature and location of the defects
- If an owner association, may identify residences
- If seeking redress through customer service under a warranty, this does not satisfy the requirements of this section.

## Proof Required-Section 942

To make a claim, the owner or owner association *only* needs to show that the home does not meet the applicable standards. No further proof of damage or causation is required.

## Damages-Section 944

- Cost of repairing any violation of the standards
- Cost of removing and replacing any improper repair by the builder
- Relocation and storage expenses
- Lost business income if the home was a place of business
- Reasonable investigative costs for each established violation
- All other costs and fees recoverable by contract or statute

## "TRUST ME … I'M THE BUILDER" & ELEVEN DECONSTRUCTED BUILDERS' MYTHS

### 1. BUILDERS' COMMENT:

*This is not a defect. It's a normal crack. Stucco and concrete slabs always crack and roofs, windows, and doors leak. It's typical as a house settles in.*

**OUR RESPONSE:** Don't believe it. While hairline cracks may occur, these cracks can and often do increase in size with time and can be caused by poorly compacted or expansive soils, structural problems, poor construction practices, or defective materials and products. Also, windows, roofs, and skylights should never leak. If any of these things occur, photograph them over time and watch how they change in size and character.

### 2. BUILDERS' COMMENT:

*Don't worry, I've fixed your problems.*

**OUR RESPONSE:** Builders, their customer service staff, and repair contractors rarely fix the underlying problem. They will, patch, plug, caulk and paint over just about anything. Before you know it, the problem reappears and your time to file an action has lapsed. Builders will never replace and will never tell you what's really causing the roof to leak, plumbing to fail or electrical fixtures to flicker. The builders make "Band Aid" or cosmetic repairs time and time again.

### 3. BUILDERS' COMMENT:

*Your one-year warranty is up, you're out of time.*

**OUR RESPONSE:** The typical builder provided written warranty is one very small measure of protection. Owners may have up to ten years after home completion to seek damages for defects. In California, SB 800 (Civil Code Section 895) identifies several time periods to bring a claim or loose it, some starting as early as 1 to 2 years after escrow closes. Also, watch out for the three-year statute from the date you discover any defect because it may trigger a need to take action before ten years.

## 4. BUILDERS' COMMENT:

*You have an extended 10 year warranty backed by insurance that will cover all workmanship or material defects in your home.*

**OUR RESPONSE:** Hogwash. These written warranties are often **not** worth the paper they're written on. Most of these warranties are nothing more than a sophisticated marketing scheme intended to sell you a new home. These policies rarely provide protection for any significant defects. Read the fine print. How it defines a defect follows no respected industry standards.

## 5. BUILDERS' COMMENT:

*You have no claim because your city building inspectors have signed off on your home as meeting all building codes.*

**OUR RESPONSE:** Building inspectors never have the time to inspect every home or all of the common areas in your development to see if they meet all building codes. Most only have time to do cursory inspections. Don't be fooled. It is no defense that the building inspection department has signed off on your home. The City has immunity from such claims.

## 6. BUILDERS' COMMENT:

*Your property will be tied up for years in a lawsuit.*

**OUR RESPONSE:** Ninety percent of lawsuits are resolved within 24 months of filing, and of those, over ninety five percent will settle and never go to trial. Most attorneys will work on a contingency fee basis. They get paid when they win. They are motivated to expedite a settlement. Don't be fooled by hourly lawyers with little or no track record and unwilling to take on the risk by financing the lawsuit. It may take them years (3-5) to resolve your case, leaving you with a hefty bill.

## 7. BUILDERS' COMMENT:

*If you file a lawsuit, you will have to disclose that you have defects and the value of your house or condo will suffer.*

**OUR RESPONSE:** Don't panic. Building defects are common. Savvy real estate agents and property management representatives know how to deal with disclosures and financing if you have to sell before the case is resolved. It is the defects in your home that must be disclosed. The builder, not you, caused the problem. The sooner you file, the quicker the settlement and the faster you receive money to fix the defects. Once the lawsuit is dismissed, the stigma quickly diminishes, and your duty to disclose diminishes with time but continues if you don't fix the problems.

## 8. BUILDERS' COMMENT:

*You'll never get a dime from me, I'm out of business (or went bankrupt) and my corporation was only a shell with no assets.*

**OUR RESPONSE:** All builders have liability insurance and most require their general and subcontractors to obtain additional insurance if a builder is sued for construction defects. Whether the builder is solvent, bankrupt, or out of business, insurance is available from the time when the damage first appears and will cover the builder and defend any lawsuit.

## 9. BUILDERS' COMMENT:

*You don't need to hire an independent expert. We're the experts. We built your home, we know what's wrong with it, and we'll fix it.*

**OUR RESPONSE:** Why would you trust the person who caused the problem in the first place to come back and fix it correctly? Without someone independent of the builder to first investigate the cause of the problem and provide a *proper* fix, you'll never know if the repair is permanent. Many construction defect law firms can arrange independent inspections free of charge. And don't just rely on the repair contractor, hire a good consultant first to diagnose the problem.

## 10. BUILDERS' COMMENT:

*Construction defect lawyers go around soliciting owners and owner association board members and trump up frivolous claims.*

**OUR RESPONSE:** Statistically, over one-third of all homes and condos built have significant construction defects. Board members of owner associations have a fiduciary duty to investigate common area complaints, and if real, to take timely and appropriate action. Insurance companies for builders continue to pay out millions of dollars annually to fix builders' mistakes.

## 11. BUILDERS' COMMENT:

*Don't even think you will win if you sue us for defects. We will bury you.*

**OUR RESPONSE:** Experienced construction defect attorneys will take your case on contingency, advance the significant expert costs, and take the risk if you loose. Find one that is well financed to hold their ground against any developer or insurance company with seemingly endless budgets. This is usually not the owners association's general counsel. Find a specialist.

# APPENDIX E: TOP 19 REASONS WHY BUILDERS FACE CONSTRUCTION DEFECT LAWSUITS

1. Poor or disparate customer service.

2. Inadequate construction plans and details.

3. Lack of proper supervision during construction.

4. Shortage of skilled workers.

5. Hiring based on lowest bid and hiring unqualified subcontractors.

6. Cutting corners, value engineering, and failure to follow plans.

7. Dismissing association board of director defect claims and complaints as an association maintenance issue.

8. Conflicts of interest by developer-controlled owner association board.

9. Overstating quality of home, condo, and common area amenities – promising too much/ delivering too little.

10. Failure to meet consumers' warranty expectations.

11. Not providing meeting rooms, signage, artwork, fitness centers, or other promised common area amenities.

12. Absence of owner and owner association maintenance manuals.

13. Poor developer transition to owner controlled board of directors.

14. Poor site selection – geology.

15. Building boom phenomena – on to the next project.

16. Setting reserves too low and other fiscal improprieties

17. Builder bankruptcies.

18. Failing to disclose known or suspected defects.

19. SB 800, the new sheriff in town.

# APPENDIX F:
# COMMON HIGH RISE DEFECTS

The following information was provided to The Miller Law Firm by Simpson Gumpertz & Heger (SGH), a national and award winning engineering firm. For more about them, please visit their website at www.sgh.com.

To view photo illustrations of the following discussion, please visit The Miller Law Firm's website at www.constructiondefects.com.

## Common High-Rise Construction Defects

Modern high-rise construction is subject to a number of design and construction shortfalls that can lead to problems including:
- Water Leakage
- Excessive Air Leakage
- Material Disintegration
- Insulating Glass Seal Failure
- Loss of Attachment
- Brittle Fracture
- Condensation
- Inadequate Noise Control
- Staining, Discoloration and Non-Uniformity of Color, and Reflectivity
- Excessive Heat Loss or Gain

Problems with high-rise construction have also increased with the increase in the use of materials traditionally only used on low and mid-rise construction, such as stucco and other siding materials.

## Exterior Wall Leakage:

- Stucco, masonry, and concrete cladding materials are not impermeable and are rarely uncracked. For example, stucco and concrete panels crack due to stress concentration at re-entrant corners (i.e., window openings), and due to normal structural deflections, thermal movements, shrinkage, and creep.
- Cracking in EIFS wall assemblies is a direct leakage path that can lead to significant underlying material deterioration and damage.
- External joint sealants, alone, do not provide highly reliable and durable waterproofing because of the following:
  - Organic sealants have relatively short lives due to heat aging, UV breakdown, strain-induced cracking, and degradation due to chemical reaction with adjacent materials. Inorganic sealants (silicones) have greater resistance to material degradation but are still limited by adhesion durability.
  - Sealant substrates are often incapable of maintaining a watertight bond with the sealant even if the sealant is good; watertight bond requires meticulously cleaned surfaces, absence of weak surface layers (e.g., mortar), absence of contaminants that can destroy adhesion (e.g., moisture), absence of cracks in the substrate (e.g., brick/mortar separations), and adequate surface area. The probability of consistently avoiding all these pitfalls is low.

  - Incomplete waterproofing membrane and sheet metal flashing for stucco, metal panel, and similar siding materials.

## Window and Glazed Curtain Wall Leakage:

Like their low rise and mid-rise counterparts, tall buildings include glazed openings in the exterior walls. These may be in the form of windows in an opaque wall, or monolithic glass and metal curtain wall assemblies. Problems with the design and construction of these assemblies include the following:
- Frame corners not reliably watertight:
  - corner seal may be missing
  - corner seal may rupture due to frame distortion during transportation and installation

- seal may fail due to normal sealant degradation and loss of adhesion
- shrinkage of plastic thermal breaks
- missing or incomplete end dams
- Penetrations - fasteners through sill allow leakage
- Inside glazing stops - allow water in glazing pocket to seep to inside if the glazing stop is at the same level as water in glazing pocket

**For more information on construction defects related issues:**

**Visit our website at www.constructiondefects.com**

**Email us at info@constructiondefects.com, or**

**Give us a call at 1-800-403-3332.**

3 1901 05871 3043